Led by the Spirit

Led by the Spirit

How Charismatic Is New Testament Christianity?

Victor C. Pfitzner

with Introduction by John T. Pless

CONCORDIA PUBLISHING HOUSE · SAINT LOUIS

Dedicated in grateful recognition to
Pastor Carl Julius Pfitzner, father, first mentor, benefactor;
and Professor Karl Heinrich Rengstorf, doctor-father, guide, friend

150th Anniversary
1869 2019
Concordia
Publishing House

Founded in 1869 as the publishing arm of The Lutheran Church—Missouri Synod, Concordia Publishing House gives all glory to God for the blessing of 150 years of opportunities to provide resources that are faithful to the Holy Scriptures and the Lutheran Confessions.

Published 2019 by Concordia Publishing House
3558 S. Jefferson Ave., St. Louis, MO 63118-3968
1-800-325-3040 • cph.org

Manufactured in the United States of America

3 4 5 6 7 8 9 10 11 29 28 27 26 25

CONTENTS

INTRODUCTION

When *Led by the Spirit: How Charismatic Is New Testament Christianity?* was published in 1976, the Charismatic or Neo-Pentecostal Movement was having a broad impact in denominations in North America, Europe, and Australia. Pfitzner's careful exegetical study was written with this phenomenon in view. While the influence of this movement has waned in the Global North, Pentecostalism and its offshoots in the Charismatic Movement continue to be a major challenge in South America, Asia, and Africa. The need to provide a Lutheran response to Pentecostalism and Neo-Pentecostalism anchored in the Holy Scriptures and faithful to the testimony of the Lutheran Confessions prompted the republishing of Dr. Pfitzner's book for use in a course in the Lutheran Leadership Development Program. Others—especially missionaries—will find this work useful as well.

Henning Wrogemann observes that it is difficult to make statements that accurately portray the whole of Pentecostalism. "This complex phenomenon actually comprises a whole range of movements."[1] Wrogemann does conclude that the Pentecostal Movement, which numbers more than five hundred million people worldwide, does display three defining characteristics: (1) the working of the Holy Spirit is tangibly experienced; (2) this experience leads to a distinct turning point in one's life; and (3) the presence of an intense missionary impulse.[2]

Although speaking in tongues was practiced in some nineteenth-century groups, modern Pentecostalism is usual identified as an outgrowth of the Wesleyan Holiness Movement in the early twentieth century. Historians point to Charles Fox Parham at Bethel Bible College in Topeka, Kansas—where Agnes Ozman spoke in tongues on January 1, 1901—and the Azusa Street Revival in Los Angeles associated with William Joseph Seymour as the origin of the movement. These two events would provide impetus toward the founding of numerous Pentecostal denominations that would form the Pentecostal Fellowship of North America (PFNA) in 1948. Pentecostalism generally held to a double work of grace (justification and sanctification) followed by a "baptism in the Spirit" evidenced by speaking in tongues. The capacity of the believer to perform miraculous signs and wonders was seen as confirmation of the Spirit's power.[3]

Pentecostalism would also make inroads into mainstream Protestant churches as well as the Roman Catholic Church by means of what would become known as the Charismatic Movement. It was newsworthy in 1960 when Dennis Bennett (1917–91), an Episcopal priest at St. Mark's Church in Van Nuys, California, began speaking in tongues and writing about his experience of the Holy Spirit. Another Californian, Larry Christenson (1928–2017), a pastor of an American Lutheran

---

1 Henning Wrogemann, *Theologies of Mission*, trans. Karl E. Böhmer, vol. 2 of *Intercultural Theology* (Downers Grove, IL: InterVarsity Press, 2018), 235.

2 Wrogemann, *Theologies of Mission*, 237.

3 For a helpful historical overview of Pentecostalism, see Walter J. Hollenweger, "Pentecostalism," and Jackie David Johns, "Pentecostal Churches," in *The Encyclopedia of Christianity*, eds. Erwin Fahlbusch et al (Grand Rapids: Eerdmans, 2003), 4:144–51, 137–44.

Church congregation in San Pedro, California, was introduced to speaking in tongues while visiting an Assemblies of God Church. Christenson would emerge as the leader of the Charismatic Movement within the Lutheran churches, authoring the books *Speaking in Tongues* and *Charismatic Renewal among Lutherans*. Within Roman Catholic circles, Francis MacNutt and Killian O'Donnell became proponents of speaking in tongues and miraculous healings.

Pentecostalism would spread into South America, Asia, and Africa as a force to be reckoned with in these settings. Pentecostalism in the Global South is diverse, often incorporating aspects of indigenous religious practices. Yet it has a common motif marked by ecstatic spiritual experience and an emphasis on the miraculous intervention of the Spirit not only in healings but also in the bestowal of material gifts, that is, the so-called "prosperity gospel." Popularized by "televangelists" in the United States, this belief holds that God will bless the faithful with wealth and health. This false theology would also be exported to the Southern Hemisphere, often associating itself with dynamic personalities who would gather devoted followers attracted by the promise that obedient faith would pay dividends in the deliverance from poverty and need.

The marks of Pentecostalism can also be seen in churches not formally identified with the movement. For example, the Ethiopian Evangelical Church Mekane Yesus has experienced the effects of Pentecostalism in its worship practices. Pentecostalism has become ecumenical in that it is not confined to the historic denominations associated with the movement such as the Assemblies of God, but it reaches into a wide spectrum of churches in the Global South.

A primary concern for Lutherans is the unity of God's Word and Spirit.[4] Lutheran theology recognizes in Pentecostalism a schism between the Word and Spirit. Exegetically, Pfitzner has demonstrated that the Holy Spirit works through the preaching of Christ crucified to build and keep His Church. The Spirit is not to be found in spectacular displays of power but in the words of the Lord both preached and written by His inspiration in the Holy Scriptures. A Lutheran critique of Pentecostalism proceeds from this biblical perspective.

The Lutheran focus is on Christ's own words about the Holy Spirit. On the eve of His crucifixion, Jesus promises to send the Comforter, the Spirit of Truth (John 14:15–17). The Holy Spirit is the "Helper" who bears witness about Christ (John 15:26). He will convict the world of sin, righteousness, and judgment

4 Here see Jeffrey Silcock: "The Holy Spirit in his freedom has bound himself to the letters of the Bible so that any demonstration of the Spirit and power today (1 Cor. 2:4) will happen in no other way than 'in and *through* the prophetic and apostolic Word that is sure, certain, and utterly reliable' (Bayer)" ("Luther on the Holy Spirit and His Use of God's Word," in *The Oxford Handbook of Martin Luther's Theology*, ed. Robert Kolb et al [Oxford: Oxford University Press, 2014], 306). Also note Werner Klän: "Within the horizon of Lutheran theology on the means of grace, the (external) Word and God's Spirit are attached inseparably to the 'lettered' word, as the Holy Spirit binds himself this word" ("God's Word as the Place Where God Dwells," in *From Wittenberg to the World: Essays on the Reformation and Its Legacy in Honor of Robert Kolb*, ed. Charles Arand et al [Göttingen: Vandenhoeck & Ruprecht, 2018], 265). Klän's whole chapter is well worth reading in light of the fact that the Lutheran argument against Pentecostalism is, at least in part, concerning the question of where is God "located."

(John 16:4–11). He will not call attention to Himself but will take what belongs to Christ and preach it (John 16:12–15). Luther writes in his exposition of John 16 (1537):

> Here Christ makes the Holy Spirit a Preacher. He does so to prevent one from gaping toward heaven in search of Him, as the fluttering spirits and enthusiasts do, and from divorcing Him from the oral Word or the ministry. One should know and learn that He will be in and with the Word, that it will guide us into all truth, in order that we may believe it, use it as a weapon, be preserved by it against all the lies and deceptions of the devil, and prevail in all trials and temptations. . . . The Holy Spirit wants this truth which He is to impress into our hearts to be so firmly fixed that reason and all one's own thoughts and feelings are relegated to the background. He wants us to adhere solely to the Word and to regard it as the only truth. And through this Word alone He governs the Christian Church to the end. (*Luther's Works* 24:362)

In the words of Steven Paulson: "The Holy Spirit's proper work is given a Christological fixation."[5]

God's Word and Spirit go together. We do not have one without the other: "By the word of the LORD the heavens were made, and by the breath of His mouth all their host" (Ps. 33:6 ESV). The Lord's breath is His Spirit (*ruach*). The breath of His mouth "is emitted when the word is spoken."[6] So in the New Testament Word and Spirit (breath and wind) go together as we see from John 3:8; 20:19–23; Acts 2:1–2. It is this Holy Spirit who works in and through the words of the Gospel to bring unbelievers to faith, the dead to life (see Eph. 2:1–22), and to keep them united with their Lord in His Church. Without the working of the Spirit in the Gospel, no one can confess Jesus Christ is Lord (see 1 Cor. 12:3).[7]

It is this scriptural teaching that is presented in the Lutheran Confessions. Luther's explanation of the Third Article in the Small Catechism is the clear confession of 1 Cor. 12:3 as he states: "I believe that I cannot by my own reason or strength believe in Jesus Christ my Lord, or come to Him; but the Holy Spirit has called me by the Gospel, enlightened me with His gifts, sanctified and kept me in the true faith." Likewise in the Large Catechism, Luther asserts:

> Neither you nor I could ever know anything about Christ, or believe in him and receive him as Lord, unless these were offered to us and bestowed on our hearts through the preaching of the gospel by the Holy Spirit. The work is finished and completed; Christ has acquired and won the treasure for us by his sufferings, death, and resurrection, etc. But if the work remained hidden so that no one knew of it, it would have all been in vain, all lost. In order that this treasure might not remain buried but be put to use and enjoyed, God has caused the Word to be published and proclaimed,

5 Steven Paulson, *Lutheran Theology* (London: T&T Clark, 2011), 197.

6 Hans Joachim Kraus, *Psalms 1–59: A Continental Commentary*, trans. Hilton C. Oswald (Minneapolis: Fortress Press, 1988), 376.

7 For more on 1 Cor. 12:3, see the essay by Hermann Sasse, "*Kyrios*," in *The Lonely Way*, Vol. 1: *1927–1939*, ed. Matthew C. Harrison (St. Louis: Concordia, 2001), 61–67.

> in which he has given the Holy Spirit to offer and apply to us this treasure, this redemption. Therefore being made holy is nothing else than bringing us to the Lord Christ to receive this blessing, to which we could not have come by ourselves.[8]

Article V of the Augsburg Confession tells us how this[9] is done: "To obtain such faith God instituted the office of preaching, giving the gospel and the sacraments. Through these, as through means, he gives the Holy Spirit who produces faith, where and when he wills, in those who hear the gospel."[10]

Therefore the Lutheran Confessions reject every form of Enthusiasm, that is, the effort to find the Spirit apart from God's Word:

> In these matters, which concern the spoken, external Word, it must be firmly maintained that God gives no one his Spirit or grace apart from the external Word which goes before. We say this to protect ourselves from the enthusiasts, that is, the "spirits," who boast that they have the Spirit apart from and before contact with the Word. On this basis they judge, interpret, and twist the Scriptures or oral Word according to their pleasure.[11]

Oswald Bayer rightly says, "Those who search for the Holy Spirit inside themselves, in realms too deep for words to express, will find ghosts, not God."[12]

In contrast to every form of spiritualist enthusiasm which we encounter in our world, we have the sure and certain promise of Jesus, who says, "The words that I have spoken to you are spirit and life" (John 6:63 ESV). His Spirited-words do what they say even as they say what they do. They bring to faith, they build up the Church in truth, and they strengthen His people for a life of witness and service in the world. The Spirit's manifold gifts are given not for the acquisition of power, personal gain, or emotional excitement but to bring Christ into focus full and clear as the Lord who lives and reigns eternally as our Savior.

John T. Pless
Assistant Professor of Pastoral Ministry and Mission
Concordia Theological Seminary, Fort Wayne, Indiana
Day of Saint Matthew, Apostle and Evangelist, 2019

---

8 Large Catechism II 38–39 (Robert Kolb and Timothy J. Wengert, eds., *The Book of Concord: The Confessions of the Evangelical Lutheran Church* [Minneapolis: Fortress, 2000], 436).

9 For more on Enthusiasm, see Regin Prenter, *Spiritus Creator: Luther's Concept of the Holy Spirit*, trans. John M. Jensen (Philadelphia: Fortress Press, 1953), 205–305; Carter Lindberg, *The Third Reformation? Charismatic Movements and the Lutheran Tradition* (Macon: Mercer University Press, 1983); Amy Nelson Burnett, "Luther and the *Schwärmer*," in *The Oxford Handbook of Martin Luther's Theology*, ed. Robert Kolb et al (Oxford: Oxford University Press, 2014), 511–24.

10 Augsburg Confession V 1–2 (Kolb and Wengert, *The Book of Concord*, 40).

11 Smalcald Articles III III 3 (Kolb and Wengert, *The Book of Concord*, 322).

12 Oswald Bayer, *Theology the Lutheran Way*, trans. Jeffrey G. Silcock and Mark C. Mattes (Grand Rapids: Eerdmans, 2007), 55.

PREFACE

There are 'head books' and 'heart books': those which have as their primary purpose the imparting of knowledge and information, the stirring of the intellect; and those which, while giving information, set out rather to inspire and stir the emotions. There are 'head books' which analyse poetry in a scholarly and objective manner; but these are preceded by the 'heart books' of the poetry itself.

This book seeks to speak to both the head and the heart. It begins from the standpoint that every experience of the Spirit of God involves the whole person of the one who is led by the Spirit (Rom. 8:14). Our Christian understanding (with the head) of God's gracious Spirit is part and parcel of our very experience (with the heart) of the Gospel itself.

But we must always realize that the Spirit of God exists before and beyond our understanding or experience. He is a reality beyond full human comprehension; He cannot be limited or shaped by human experience. That is why this study sets out to explore the wonderful mystery of the Spirit on the basis of God's own Word and not on the basis of human experience.

If this book tends to speak more to the head than to the heart, this bias has been deliberately chosen. Charismatic writers, both Pentecostal and neo-Pentecostal, claim to base their theology of the Spirit on the Scriptures. And those who oppose the charismatics make the same claim. How, then, can the differing conclusions be explained? Any reading of charismatic literature will soon make clear that it appeals strongly to the 'experience of the Spirit' as proof of the truth of its claims. In turn, Scripture itself is read and understood in the light of that experience. What we obviously need is a clear biblical hermeneutic (that is, how the Bible is meant to be read and understood), as well as a clear understanding of the nature of Christian experience and its relationship to the Scriptures.

While this study from time to time adopts a polemical tone, its purpose is positive, not negative. It does not seek to attack charismatics for the sake of polemics. The study of the power and person of the Holy Spirit is a study of the grace and mercy of God, of His love in Jesus Christ. To be led by the Spirit means to be led into the glorious liberty of the children of God, to a joyful understanding and living of the Gospel.

The chapters of this book are, to some extent, based on papers and talks presented to various groups in the Lutheran Church of Australia. They include sections of a paper delivered to the Fourth General Convention of that Church at Horsham, Victoria, in October 1972, as well as lectures offered to an in-service training-school for pastors of the South Australia District of the Church in May 1972. Both these past papers and the present study were requested in view of the challenge, and often confusion, caused by the charismatic or neo-Pentecostal movement within the major denominations, including the Lutheran Church.

It will be obvious to anyone who has read some of the many recent books dealing with the Spirit and His gifts, that the present writer is indebted to many fruitful minds. In particular, indebtedness to Frederick D. Bruner, Charles K. Barrett, James D. G. Dunn, Kurt Koch, Anthony A. Hoekema, Paul Barnett, and Peter Jensen is gratefully acknowledged. Footnotes, giving detailed textual arguments and literature references, have been deliberately omitted to keep the presentation as simple as possible.

Every effort has been made to keep the study clear and intelligible, but this does not mean that the reader can escape some deep and detailed study of the Scriptures. The discipline of thorough searching of God's revelation is one of the marks of spiritual maturity. Many may be tempted to skip the biblical study of Chapters III to VI; however, the summary of Chapter VII will, hopefully, direct the searcher for truth back to those basic studies.

My only justification for another book on the Spirit is the contention that we are never finished with the quest for the Spirit, or, better, for an understanding of His person and work. In addition, the writer confesses his allegiance to the Lutheran understanding of the Gospel, and thus believes that the Lutheran understanding of the Means of Grace (Word and Sacraments) as the 'home' of the Spirit, can help us understand and arrive at that fullness of the Spirit of which Saint Paul speaks in Ephesians 5:18. The ultimate aim of this book will be reached if it helps the reader to live as a child of God who is 'filled with all the fulness of God' (Eph. 3:19). That is the ultimate of ultimates.

Malvern,
South Australia.
August 1975

Victor C. Pfitzner.

Chapter I

THE CHALLENGE OF THE CHARISMATICS

1. Defining the Challenge

It is quite understandable that from time to time we should find a longing to return to the Early Church which enjoyed that first flush of zeal and fervency in the possession of the Spirit. But the return to the past often entails a rather naive and uncritical picture of that church.

Too often it is forgotten that there never was a perfect church. In its first days as the new people of God, the Early Church had its Ananias and Sapphira who lied to and tempted the Holy Spirit (Acts 5:3,9). It experienced petty squabbles over material things (Acts 6). Paul's missionary congregations also revealed some sad and serious flaws. The Galatians, or many among them, denied the Spirit of freedom and the gift of faith by their return to the Law (Gal. 3:2). All the errors of the congregation at Corinth ('the church of Vanity Fair' as A. M. Hunter calls it) can be summed up as an abuse of the Spirit's gifts in a loveless and boasting pride, based on their false understanding of themselves as 'spiritual people'.

Nevertheless, who can deny that the Early Church was indeed led by the Spirit? One of the chief aims of Luke in the Acts of the Apostles was just this: to show how the Spirit was involved in every important decision and every new move of the church from the Day of Pentecost onwards. And who would not want the church of today to be so guided and led?

It is just here that the Pentecostal groups since the turn of the century, and, in particular, the charismatic movement since the early 1960s, have had an unsettling impact on the main-stream churches of Christendom. They have created a considerable degree of uneasiness, instilling doubts as to whether the main-stream churches have lost something which they ought to have: a surer sense and clearer evidence of the possession of the Holy Spirit, plus such external signs as speaking in tongues.

From small beginnings in the last century, the quest for this 'experience of the Spirit' has not only produced many new denominations, but has now more recently produced a major international and inter-denominational movement—in a sense, a second ecumenical movement—which unites Christians from various confessions and traditions in what they claim is the common possession and experience of the Spirit. This 'new Reformation', as it has been called, has major ecumenical significance, since it is seen by many as one way, perhaps finally the only way, in which the old doctrinal differences, which have previously separated the various churches, are to be overcome. The catch-cry of the new enthusiast ecumenicity is thus not only 'One in Christ', but also 'One in the possession of the Spirit'. For them, that is enough to unite all Christians.

The above slogan is fine if there can be agreement on what is meant by 'the, possession of the Spirit'. But, even within the charismatic movement, there is no such thing as agreed doctrine on the Spirit and His work. While we can speak of a 'movement' in general terms, there is no consensus, no commonly-held confession, on all the varied aspects of the charismatic stance. Indeed, some of the Pentecostal churches are even unitarian, denying the doctrine of the Trinity! And while charismatics of the various historic confessions do enjoy a sort of fellowship based on a common experience of the Spirit attested by tongue-speaking, such a bond can and will never let the churches escape the task of seeking a common expression of the church's teaching and doctrine.

Before we proceed any further, it will be good to define some of the terms already used, and others yet to be used in this study. Sometimes the terms: Pentecostal, neo-Pentecostal, and charismatic are used in such a way as to create some confusion. For the sake of clarity we will use the terms in the following way:

1. **Pentecostal** is used for that movement and for those churches which have grown out of the quest for the Spirit and His tangible gifts since the turn of the century. Pentecostals see and demand the so-called 'baptism of the Spirit' as a second, separate experience of grace after conversion itself. There is general agreement among them that this will not only come subsequent to conversion, but also will be attested by some external sign, especially speaking in tongues. With some, tongues is even demanded as a sign of this 'filling' with the Spirit, and a Christian is not considered to have reached spiritual maturity without this special filling.

2. **Neo-Pentecostal** is used for that movement embracing Christians within the traditional church-bodies who, especially since the early 1960s, have desired for themselves and for their churches a greater experience of the power of the Spirit and His special gifts for ministry. These Christians stay within their denominations and usually do not accept all the emphases and excesses of Pentecostal teaching. While they seek a greater experience of the Spirit for themselves and others, they still profess faithfulness to the central teachings of their churches.

3. The term **charismatic** is a more general one. It is derived from the Greek word used in the New Testament for grace (*charis*), and from the term used by Paul in 1 Corinthians 12 and 14 for 'gifts of the Spirit' (*charismata*). Thus the term charismatics is used to include both Pentecostals and neo-Pentecostals, to cover anyone who believes that the gifts of the Spirit referred to in the New Testament are just as valid and available for the believer today as they were in the Early Church.

The distinction between the first two terms is not always clearly defined. But the Pentecostal has, for example, no appreciation of the sacramental life of the church (especially of baptismal regeneration), nor does he appreciate the traditional liturgical life of the church. More importantly for Lutherans, the Pentecostal understanding of justification and sanctification and their relatedness as the work of the

Spirit must be viewed as either rejecting, or at least placing in danger, the great doctrine of the Reformation, *sola gratia* (by grace alone). Where sanctification and the quest for holiness are seen apart from grace, apart from the gift of the Spirit in justification itself, where 'tarrying' or waiting for the Spirit denies every Christian's present possession of the Spirit by faith, the free gift of the Spirit and the free Gospel are denied. We thus finish with a new legalism in the name of the Spirit.

This rejection of Pentecostalism may be regarded by some as arbitrary. However, this study is not really concerned with arguing the case with Pentecostals; a fuller and more detailed argument would be necessary to explain the above rejection of Pentecostal teaching in its most-commonly-accepted form. And yet this study will provide enough incidental evidence to illustrate the complete incompatibility between the Pentecostal teaching and that found in the New Testament.

This study is, first and foremost, concerned with the challenge to the church presented by the neo-Pentecostal movement. More particularly, it is part of a dialogue with Lutherans who claim to have already had a special experience of the Spirit, or who desire it. It is addressed also to those who want an answer to the urgent question: Am I a complete Christian without this special experience?

This is an intensely practical question for many Christians today. Many Christians are concerned about apathy and coldness within their local congregation. They may come to various conclusions as to why this apparent spiritual stagnation has set in; a lack of joyous Gospel proclamation from the pulpit, traditionalism, formalism, nominalism, secularism, and many other 'isms' may be cited as causes. Often comparisons are then made with the zeal, ardour, enthusiasm, fervency of spirit (call it what you like), lively worship, and evangelistic fervour which are usually attributed to charismatic circles. These features are often highlighted and used to throw a bad light on the anaemic, spirit-less life, worship, and piety sometimes found in congregations of the major historical denominations. Many Lutherans who have come into contact with members of the Assemblies of God or with the Full Gospel Business Men's Fellowship International (FGBMFI) have often drawn quick comparisons between Lutherans and charismatics which leave the former found wanting.

Whether such comparisons are always fair need not be argued here—though it can be said that Lutherans (and many other Christians) have a sad habit of too easily overlooking real spiritual life and growth when they bemoan all that seems to be wrong with the church! We are simply making the point that charismatics both inside and outside the main denominations raise a vital question which demands an answer: Have the churches been guilty of quenching the Spirit, of blocking His path, of neglecting or even rejecting His special gifts? Before we attack what we believe to be the error of others, we should be ready to confess our own spiritual apathy, if that confession must be made.

And it may be necessary for the pastors of the church to make their own confession of guilt, too. The sins of God's people, as the Old Testament in particular often reminds us, are very often to be traced back to the sins of their spiritual leaders (cf. Ezek. 34).

But it is just here that soberness and not muddle-headed enthusiasm must reign. The fact that Pentecostalism has largely lost its sectarian taint (at the New Delhi World Council of Churches Assembly in 1961 several South American Pentecostal churches were admitted as members of the WCC), or the fact that neo-Pentecostalism has its followers in virtually every major denomination in Christendom, does not justify an uncritical 'jumping on the band-waggon' of the new Spirit-movement. Among all the threats which face the church, those which arise from within are perhaps even more dangerous than those which come from outside. False teaching is heresy, even if it uses traditional Christian terminology, whenever it distorts the faith of the church as expressed in its creeds and confessions.

2. Theology and the Whole Truth

If there is something to be learned from the charismatics, or if we have to reject some of their teachings, we must be clear that both actions are based on sound theology.

Such a seemingly-obvious statement requires brief clarification. Too often the new is immediately rejected because it is just that. Because the church by its very nature is bound closely to a long tradition, it is easier to stick to traditional formulations, structures, organizations, and accepted practice than to adopt new ideas and ways. That which we have not tried, or which we have not fully understood, is often pushed aside with an easy label condemning it as a dangerous 'ism'. For example, a call for small-cell-group activity, whether for prayer, Bible study, or some form of mutual edification, can, by those who do not wish to understand or to become involved, be branded as 'Pentecostal'. But to be led by the Spirit means being open to the Word even if this means something new or untried. There is a great need in our congregations for open, earnest seeking of the truth together, and for a readiness to listen lovingly to one another in obedience to that Word.

On the other hand, searching for the truth under the Spirit always involves pinpointing dangerous errors. That is the Spirit in loving action. Unfolding the truth and unmasking error go hand in hand.

It is worth remembering that most of the New Testament writings arose from the Early Church's struggle against error. And the interesting thing about this struggle is that the people against whom the New Testament writers had to pen their lines did not always appear as raving heretics mouthing blasphemies and patent lies. On the contrary, the early converts were impressed by such heretics because they presented very plausible arguments, and seemed to be orthodox and pious in their contentions. The call back to the Law on the part of the Judaizers who were threatening the liberty of the

Galatians would have appeared as orthodoxy itself! And the claims of the Corinthian errorists to be 'spiritual people' surely touched on a central truth.

The Apostle Paul in both these cases had to brand false teaching for what it was: heresy. But he also had to do something rather more difficult: he had to show quite clearly how such superficially attractive ideas were a denial of the Gospel because of their implications or logical consequences. For example, Paul felt quite free to circumcise his pupil and co-worker, Timothy. He had nothing against the old rite as such. If it helped him in his approach to the Jews, well and good; for the Jews he would be a Jew (1 Cor. 9:20). But when this rite was seen by some as a necessary requirement for faith, or at least as a compulsory prerequisite for entrance into the church, it was rejected vigorously by Paul as a denial of the Gospel of grace. At this point he would allow no uncertainty or compromise. Either circumcision and the Law, or grace and the Gospel! The one cancelled out the other.

In the same way, in our study of the work and gifts of the Spirit, it is necessary to be on the alert for any implications which will detract from the Gospel, which offers grace as a pure gift, unmerited and unearned.

Of course, error is not merely a matter of wrong emphasis. But it is worth considering whether most ancient and modern errors in the history of the church have not resulted from distortion of the ecumenical Christian creeds. It is possible to arrange a whole series of distortions of the Gospel into three groups, each of which represents either a false understanding of, or one-sided emphasis on, one of the Creed's three articles of faith.

The First Article confesses the kingship of God as creator of all things, as well as His continuing providential care of what He has made. But a faith which sees this as the heart of the Creed can easily slip into the error of viewing the kingdom of God as the restoration of harmony in a perfect human society, in terms of human justice, peace, and goodwill for all men—and nothing more. Again, we have become increasingly aware of the fact that we are witnesses to the despoiling of God's creation. The pollution crisis and ecological dilemma have been taken up as key theological problems. But to call simply for the restoration and preservation of God's world by a responsible use of His creation is to preach only Law and not Gospel. Again, much of the new understanding of mission as aiding the so-called under-developed nations in their struggle for self-realization and economic independence, and which rejects the old concept of mission as spreading a Gospel message, also points to a distorted emphasis on the First Article in isolation from the other two.

Secondly, there is a faith and a piety which arise from an over-emphasis on the Second Article to the detriment of the other two. We need only think of the pietistic repetition of orthodox slogans and catch-cries about Jesus—a sort of 'Jesuology' which fails to relate the redemption and lordship of Christ to the work of the Father and the Holy Spirit. In this somewhat sentimental and religiously-romantic type of piety, we end up with an excessive emphasis on personal faith; there is little or no understanding of the ethic of love or of practical concern for the neighbour and for God's creation as a whole; and, above all, there is little appreciation of the nature of the church as the family of God who are gathered together in worship around Word and Sacraments. This kind of subjectivism is found also in that 'decision theology' which stresses 'my faith', 'my personal decision for Christ' to such an extent that the objective work of the Father and the Spirit in offering salvation as a free gift is blurred.

In the same way, it would be interesting to examine how a lopsided, and sometimes very wrong, understanding of the Spirit has produced various errors in the history of the church from the first century to our own. In his book, *What About Tongue Speaking?*, A. A. Hoekema has shown that a special claim to the Spirit and to manifestations of His presence and power has often been a vital part of a sectarian movement. This was certainly the case with the strange sect of Montanism and with the various Gnostic groups in the early history of the church. In our own century, the older charismatic movement of Pentecostalism is the classic example of a distortion of the Gospel through a one-sided stress on the experience of the power of the Spirit in a tangible and demonstrable form. Pentecostalism is able, with an at-first almost disarming display of conservative Protestant orthodoxy, to repeat the old evangelical Reformation formulas of the past. We hear again of the sole merits of Christ, of justification by grace; we hear again the familiar stress on the reception of grace by faith alone (even if the stress on obedience which must follow faith is more characteristic). And yet the decisive question remains: Are we still left with the full Gospel? Or does not the Pentecostal quest for the Spirit lead to a new legalism which finally detracts from and even destroys the Gospel of grace?

In the following chapters we will take another look at the biblical teaching on the Spirit, concentrating on His work and gifts. Our aim, to state the point again, is not simply to polemicize against false views, but to attempt to rediscover where the Spirit is, indeed, to be found, to rediscover His 'fullness'. But the doctrine of the Spirit, as also the reality of His presence, can never be isolated from the total truth of the Christian faith. The Spirit and the Gospel belong together; both are free gifts of God. It is through the Spirit that the believer receives the grace (*charis*) of God; it is through Him that God pours out His concrete spiritual gifts (*charismata*) for ministry and loving service in the church, and from there to the whole world.

Theology is not an academic exercise for intellectuals. We are certainly called to work out our faith and salvation with fear and trembling (Phil. 2:12), and to give a good account of the hope that is in us (1 Peter 3:15). But theology is finally the complete confessing and living of the Gospel truth which has claimed us. Melanchthon, Dr. Martin Luther's right-hand man, once wrote: 'To know Christ is to know His benefits'. We can also say: 'To know the Spirit is to know His benefits'. To know the Spirit is indeed to know and believe the

Gospel. For the study of the Spirit is really a sub-chapter in the study of the Gospel of God's loving and gracious forgiveness in His Son. We are not interested in speculation, no matter how pious, in guessing how and where the Spirit of God may be at work today in world affairs, as men search for social justice, order, and peace. Certainly God is also at work in secular affairs, for He has not abdicated His rule as king over the whole of creation. But we want to learn again where the Spirit and His benefits **can, with all certainty,** be found, so that we may become aglow with the love of God, the fruit of the Spirit, and as His little saints become parcels of grace to all men.

The Christian surely is a charismatic in the true sense of the word. Paul makes it quite clear that being a child of God means being led by the Spirit in the experience of *charis* (Rom. 8). But he also insists that **all** Christian ministry and service is charismatic, for it includes and involves the use of all the concrete and individual gifts of grace that have been supplied through the same Spirit (1 Cor. 12).

Chapter II

THE QUEST FOR THE SPIRIT—THEN AND NOW

It took the Christian church some three centuries to establish the place of the Holy Spirit in trinitarian theology. And even then the Spirit seems to have remained the forgotten or taken-for-granted member of the Trinity in the long history of faith, worship, and piety right down to our century. Certainly, the Early Church made its clear confession to the person and work of the Spirit, as clearly as it confessed its faith in Jesus as Lord and Christ. It is also interesting to note that early Christians were not restricted to the usual trinitarian order to which we are accustomed in the three historic symbols of the church—the Apostolic, Nicene, and Athanasian Creeds. As well as the usual order of Father-Son-Spirit (Matt. 28:19), we also find the order Spirit-Lord-God (1 Cor. 12:4–7; Eph. 4:4–6), and Father-Spirit-Jesus (1 Peter 1:2). Thus it cannot be maintained that the Early Church was responsible for pushing the Spirit into the background, into a kind of third-class membership in the Trinity.

1. The Neglected Doctrine

And yet the Spirit remained neglected in Christian theology in subsequent centuries. This can be only partly explained by the fact that in the New Testament (as well as the Old Testament) the Spirit remains very much a mystery. Jesus is acclaimed with many Christological titles (such as Messiah, Lord, Prophet, Priest, King, Saviour, Shepherd), and some could claim to have seen Him in the flesh (John 1:14); the Spirit attracts no such treatment. The Spirit is given no great array of new titles, but is simply known as God in His saving and life-giving presence, with certain signs of that presence. The only new title given to the Spirit in the New Testament is that of *Paraclete* in the Gospel according to St. John. But the exact meaning of that title is not even clear. Does it mean Admonisher, Comforter, or Advocate—or even a combination of all three ideas?

However, despite the mystery of His person and the mystery of His coming at Pentecost, one thing is certain: the Early Church knew itself to be God's people in possession of the promised Spirit of God. Everything that they were, all they possessed and hoped for as God's saints, came to them via that Spirit who was also the Spirit of Christ. The well-known New Testament scholar, C. K. Barrett, goes so far as to say:

> 'No more certain statement can be made about the Christians of the first generation than this: they believed themselves to be living under the immediate government of the Spirit of God' (*The Holy Spirit and the Gospel Tradition*, p. 1).

Why then did it take the church so long to develop a doctrine of the Holy Spirit? The first ecumenical council at Nicaea in A.D. 325, while developing a doctrine on the equality of the Son with the Father ('of one substance with the Father'), did not as yet develop any parallel statement about the person of the Spirit and His relationship to the other persons of the Trinity. There was as yet no actual Third Article as found in the Western creed, based on the old Roman baptismal confession, and which became known as the Apostles Creed. The original Nicene Creed simply confesses at the end: 'And *[we believe]* in the Holy Spirit'.

It was only at the second ecumenical council at Constantinople in A.D. 381 that this brief statement was lengthened to the form of confession familiar to us today:

> 'And I believe in the Holy Spirit, the Lord and giver of life, who proceeds from the Father . . . , who together with the Father and the Son is worshipped and glorified, who spoke by the prophets'.

The only other later addition to this brief confession was the famous filioque which confesses that the Spirit proceeds from the Father and the Son—an addition still not accepted by the Eastern Orthodox Church.

That the person and work of the Spirit was not entirely neglected in the early centuries of the church can be seen from the 'frozen dogma' contained in the church's liturgies, hymns, and prayers. But even here it is worth noting that the Eastern Orthodox churches still do not have any solemn liturgical prayers directed to the Spirit. Even the so-called *epiklesis*, or 'calling down' of the Spirit, found in the eucharistic liturgy, is really a prayer directed to the Father to send down His Spirit with all His gifts. It is consequently with good reason that one noted church-historian, Dr. H. Sasse, has spoken of the teaching on the Holy Spirit as 'one of the uncompleted doctrines of the Church'. It is interesting to speculate whether later ecumenical councils (at Ephesus in A.D. 431 and Chalcedon in A.D. 451) would have developed more fully the doctrine of the Spirit if the church at that time had possessed more theological energy instead of being enervated by the political events of the time, especially the Germanic invasion of the Roman Empire.

2. The Quest for the Spirit in the New Testament World

Historians and students of New Testament times might argue that the early Christians did not feel called on to explain what they meant by the Spirit, and this for several reasons. After all, an outsider looking into the church could see that there was a spiritual power at work among these Christians, a supernatural power without which the growth of the church could not be adequately explained. All he had to do was to join these Christians to experience the power of the Spirit! And since the Early Church gained many of its converts either from the Jewish synagogue or from those pagans who had come under the influence of the synagogue (in the New Testament they are called 'God-fearers', those who had accepted the Old Testament monotheism and the Jewish ethical system), there was little need to explain who the person of the Spirit was. This could be presupposed from their knowledge of the Old Testament.

On the other hand, the early missionaries like Saint Paul could just as easily presuppose that their pagan hearers would not challenge the reality of a spiritual world and of spiritual powers. It could indeed be—and this seems to have been the case in the congregation at Corinth—that some of the confusion over the Spirit arose because converts did not easily and immediately shake off the heathen ideas of supernatural power which belonged to their former life. This much is at least clear. The religions and philosophies of the Roman-Hellenistic world, the world of New Testament times, accepted and presupposed far more readily than does our present world the existence of spiritual reality over against material reality.

It is important that we read the New Testament teaching on the Spirit within the context of the contemporary world and its ideas. The Greek word *pneuma* can mean wind, breath, or spirit (English words such as 'pneumatic' and 'pneumonia' are derived from the Greek word), and was used from early Greek times to describe the breath of life in animate creatures. In contrast to the body, it also denoted the psychological or spiritual entity in man. Classical Greek literature does not know the phrase 'holy spirit', but in later Hellenistic* literature in particular, *pneuma* was used to describe the highest divine being, the ultimate spiritual power, as well as other non-corporeal, supernatural beings, whether good or evil.

Hellenistic and Jewish thought in New Testament times showed a special interest in the spiritual world—a development which can be explained in the following way. The old gods of Greek paganism had been actually conceived as super-humans, closely related to mankind; they had lived close to earth above Mount Olympus, and even behaved like humans with all their foibles and failings. However, in Hellenistic times these ancient gods no longer possessed any real power or reality in the mind of the average man. The course of history, with its endless human wrangling for power, rather suggested that this world was subject to other powers, such as fate and fortune. No wonder, then, that *Fortuna* was one of the most important deities in the Roman-Hellenistic world and the official guardian of many a city. No wonder that people, even emperors like Tiberius, in whose reign our Lord lived and was crucified, turned to astrology and magic in an attempt to discover the purpose of life and its control.

At the same time philosophers were speculating increasingly about a highest spiritual being (just as early philosophers like Socrates and Plato had been able to speak of 'god' as an ultimate reality and power). But—and this is the important point—the world of ultimate reality, of final truth, of the spirit, was seen as far removed from this world. Where previously the gods were immanent (close to man), now they were viewed as transcendent (far removed). Thus Hellenistic religions and philosophies were all engaged in a quest for union with the

* The adjective 'Hellenistic' describes that culture which was an amalgam or mixture of Greek and Eastern civilization, which resulted from Alexander the Great's conquest of the Eastern Mediterranean world as far east as India.

spiritual world, in an attempt to bridge the great chasm between the divine and the human.

Truth was seen not so much as that which could be discovered by reason or philosophy, but as that which had to be revealed. Revelations from such famous oracles as the Sibyl at Cumae, or the prophetess of Apollo at Delphi, assumed great importance, and were gathered into large collections.

Even the most popular philosophy in the Roman Empire in New Testament times, Cynic-Stoic Popular Moral Philosophy, while seeming to base all its arguments on human reason, still illustrates the quest for the spirit that we have been talking about. Here the problem of God's transcendence is wiped out with one stroke. 'God' is nothing else than 'nature', or the natural law of reason which pervades the whole universe and which is found as a spark of the divine in each person. Man finds his role and purpose in life when he learns to follow the spirit of the divine within him, and lives in harmony with nature. This is pantheism in its classical form. The spirit is naturally within man. That this picture of man has nothing at all in common with the biblical picture of man, who is naturally 'flesh' and without the Spirit of God, is obvious.

In general, it can be said that in Hellenistic thinking man is essentially of two parts, flesh and spirit, or body and soul. The moral philosophy of Paul's day, as well as the many mystery-cults which sprang up in Hellenistic times, saw man as a miniature of the universe in which the spirit is to be contrasted with matter. The body was viewed as the prison of the soul or spirit, which was the noble element in man, directly related to the world of ultimate spiritual reality. In the mystery-cults the spirit was often viewed as a kind of supernatural substance which took hold of a man to renew him and stamp him as divine, assured of immortality. Man's spirit is finally divine, and needs to be released from the shackles of matter, of fate, and of the body with all its desires and passions. We will see later that some of this kind of thinking lay behind the problems at Corinth which Paul had to set in order, and influenced how Paul spoke of the Spirit of God over against that early error in the church known as Gnosticism.

The union of the spirit of man with the divine was also seen as the highest goal by the Hellenistic Jewish thinker, Philo of Alexandria. For Philo, of course, the Highest Good with which man is to be united is the God of the Old Testament. But the Hellenistic influences on Philo's thought are very strong. The gap between man and the transcendent God is so wide that it must be bridged by intermediaries. In Jewish inter-testamental thought we find a new (compared with the Old Testament) interest in angelic and demonic beings, probably as a result of eastern dualistic influences. We also find in Philo and Rabbinic literature the picture of a God who is so far removed from man that even the Law had to be given to Moses via intermediaries, through the agency of angelic beings. Paul reflects this thought in Gal. 3:19,20 (see also Acts 7:38 in Stephen's speech).

The above sketchy comments will be enough to suggest that Paul, to cite one New Testament writer, made statements about the Holy Spirit which have a significance that is greater than we at first might suspect. Indeed, his teaching can often be fully understood only if seen against the background of Hellenistic thinking and in contrast to it. For example, imagine how startling to the Greek ear certain of his statements might have seemed: that the Corinthian Christians' bodies were 'members of Christ' (not just their renewed spirits, 1 Cor. 6:15), that the believer's 'body is a temple of the Holy Spirit' (and not some shackle that the soul or spirit must cast off or escape in order to gain eternal life, 1 Cor. 6:19)! How un-Hellenistic was his appeal to the Romans to 'present your bodies as a living sacrifice, . . . which is your spiritual worship' (Rom: 12:1)!

With Paul, as with the rest of the New Testament, the work of the Spirit is never linked with the human spirit as the better, higher, more noble, or purer part of man. Without the Holy Spirit of God, man in his totality as body, soul, and spirit is totally 'flesh' (*sarx*), and that means, in Pauline diction, a sinner under divine judgment of death.

Paul's teaching on the Spirit is strikingly *somatic* (*soma* = body). The Spirit binds believers into the Body of Christ (1 Cor. 12:13), and shows His presence in tangible ways in the physical, corporeal world, in a life of obedience. He will also be active at the resurrection in the creation of new 'spiritual bodies' in contrast to the old 'natural bodies' (1 Cor. 15:44–46). The experience of the Spirit and His power does not lead to mystical flights into the supernatural, away from the material world, but places the believer under the lordship of Christ within the normal conditions of his physical existence.

3. The Problem of Religious Experience

We have several times used the phrase 'experience of the Spirit'. New Testament Greek has no word for 'experience' (the AV does use this term to translate the Greek word *dokimē* in Rom. 5:4, but the RSV translation 'character' is far better, since the original suggests that which has been tried, tested, and found true). Paul certainly had an important experience on the Damascus road, one which changed the whole course of his life. His vision of the risen Lord meant both his conversion and his call to be an apostle to the Gentiles. But he never used this experience to prove anything but his call to be an apostle (see 1 Cor. 9:1; 15:8–10; Gal. 1:16). To those who, like true Hellenists, demanded proof of his spiritual authority with demonstrations of supernatural power, he boasted of his weakness in order that God might be glorified. He even refused to make anything of that ecstatic experience which he had been granted, but spoke instead of his 'thorn . . . in the flesh' (2 Cor. 12:1–10), boasting only in God's 'power made perfect in weakness'. When the Corinthians expected from him a message of obvious supernatural wisdom and power expounded with brilliant oratory, he continued to point to the message of the Cross as the only power of God through the Spirit (1 Cor. 1:18–2:16). When they demanded proof (*dokimē* again) that Christ was speaking in him, he pointed only to the crucified Lord as the source of power, and suggested that (as in his own case) his readers would be powerful only as long as the crucified Christ lived in them (2 Cor. 13:3–5).

Paul, who worked miracles, who could speak in tongues and cite visions, never saw or used these experiences as confirmation of the truth of his message. His Gospel was the same as that which the other apostles preached. He stood within the teaching tradition of the Early Church, and from time to time could cite that tradition in order to remind his readers of a forgotten truth. 1 Cor. 11:23 and 15:1 introduce such pieces of fixed tradition and use the standard technical terms (found in Rabbinic teaching) to introduce a tradition that has been passed on in an unbroken succession. Power was for him not that which God had vested in him, but rather that which the Spirit had vested in the message of the Gospel (1 Cor. 1:18; 2:4,5).

These comments on the New Testament setting with its quest for the Spirit open up new insights in our attempt to understand the quest for the Spirit and the experience of His power in our own age. It can quickly be demonstrated that the charismatic movement owes much (if not most) of its appeal to its claim that the experience of the Spirit in a tangible way transforms a Christian's faith and life. Two quotations will suffice to illustrate this point.

Rev. Dennis Bennett, the American Episcopalian minister whose neo-Pentecostal writings have had a great impact also in Australia (see his *Nine O'Clock in the Morning* and *The Holy Spirit and You*), says:

> 'The church is in a mess, organized Christianity a failure. Why? Because the Holy Spirit has not had a fair chance to work **experientially** in the church . . . **It is time** to stop relying on intellectual analyses and **to start relying on spiritual experience.** After all Christianity is not an intellectual matter at all. It is a purely personal and spiritual matter' (*emphasis mine*).

Ignoring for the moment the more-than-doubtful definition of Christianity in this statement, what interests us is the prime role played by experience. This typically-charismatic view is underlined by the equally-noted American Lutheran neo-Pentecostal, Larry Christenson, who writes in *Speaking in Tongues*, p. 14:

> 'The **experience** of "speaking in tongues" has intensified the **sense** of the presence of God; the Word of God has become **more contemporary, believable**; Christ the Lord has become **more real**—in a word, faith has been strengthened' (*emphasis again mine*).

Now we should not cheaply attack the appeal to Christian experience as such. Christian faith is, indeed, more than intellectual assent to a series of doctrinal propositions; it also means trust, a personal relationship with God and with Christ, which involves the experience of grace. But what is very disconcerting, and certainly not found in the New Testament, is the idea that **experience substantiates the truth and reality of faith.** In the New Testament, faith is always directed to Christ who is found in the Word, not to Christ found in a personal and private experience.

But, before we analyse charismatic experience more closely (we shall return to this later in the study), we should note that the appeal to experience is a phenomenon of our age. It is completely understandable that the charismatic quest for an experience of the Spirit's power and His gifts should have arisen, and continue to arise, where spiritual apathy and sterile dogmatism prevail, unrelieved by powerful Gospel-preaching, sacramental celebration, and liturgical richness. But it is a simple fact that our age, as perhaps none before, has seen a revolt against thought and rationality in favour of experience and the appeal to the emotions. Whether in the field of politics, business, or religion, the emotive appeal carries more weight than a carefully presented, logical argument. Ours is the age of catch-lines in advertising, slogans in politics, and experience in religion!

Contact with the divine or supernatural world through ecstasy* or some other metaphysical experience is a phenomenon claimed by many cults and religions throughout the world from ancient to modern times. But, although certain things still remain unexplained, today we know a little more about the physical and psychological factors involved in such experience. Psychology and medicine have begun to uncover the power of the mind over the body, and the interaction of body and mind in some mental disorders. Religious experience can sometimes be analysed in objective psychological terms, even though the experience may be subjectively very real.

Trances, dreams, visions, revelation experiences, and similar experiences, can all be induced by a variety of means. The prophets of Baal, prancing around their altar on Mt. Carmel, calling on their god and slashing themselves with sharp instruments, probably to the accompaniment of frenzied musical tones (1 Kings 18:26–29), were simply using a standard technique to induce a state of ecstasy in which their god would communicate with his devotees. Similar ecstatic states in which a prophet, seer, or shaman sees 'a vision of the divine', experiences a 'celestial journey of the soul', or in some way communes with the infinite, are still known among many cults and religions, especially in Asia. Self-inflicted pain via flagellation, the droning tones of instruments and monotonous chants, frequent repetition of sacred formulas, meditation, fasting, asceticism, and drugs are some of the means used to induce religious experience.

Anyone who has been to a pop-festival and seen the almost religious fervour (if not mania!) of screaming, clutching, frenzied teenagers who have been whipped up into a state of extreme excitement in which they openly worship their stars, will appreciate the role of appropriate music in religious experience. One could also cite the music with immediate appeal to the emotions which is characteristic of some mass-revival meetings.

Our Western world has also become more familiar with the use of meditation and drugs to induce religious experience, especially with the renewed attempts of various forms of Eastern mysticism to conquer the West. Not so long ago, Zen Buddhism was a popular philosophy, among young people in particular, offering one way of

* The word ecstasy comes from two Greek words (*ek* and *stasis*) and denotes, literally, that state in which one 'stands outside of' oneself. The ecstatic person is literally 'beside himself'. Seen from a different angle, he is one who is under an outside power or influence.

revolting against Western secularistic ideals and materialism. Various maharishis (literally 'great seers') have appeared in the Western world from the East, proclaiming new versions of mystic experience and a gospel of peace, self-realization, and union with the divine through meditation. In recent years, many internationally-known figures have dabbled in 'transcendental meditation'. And how many housewives in suburbia have diligently gone through their yoga course, faithfully carrying out their exercises, without realizing that yoga is an important part of Hindu mysticism? Anyone walking down the main streets of our cities, whether in Europe, America, or Australia, must eventually confront the saffron-robed adherents of the Divine Light Mission, ringing their bells and chanting their monotonous litanies to Krishna. What this 'church' offers is the experience of 'divine light', the vision of god within oneself. They claim to offer what Christians do not have: the final proof of the existence of god through actually seeing and **experiencing** god!

While drugs are a tragic part of our society, they represent far more than an easy escape from a reality too harsh to face without them. Drug-usage is a common feature in both ancient and modern religions, whether in Egypt, Arabia, India, China, or the two Americas. There exists today in North America a legally-incorporated church, known as the Native American Church, numbering some 225,000 Indians and some whites, who through a 'sacramental' use of the drug peyote, commune with the spirit of God (see R. E. L. Masters and Jean Houston, *The Varieties of Psychedelic Experience*, London: Turnstone Books, 1966, Ch. 2). The use of drugs by holy men can be documented from early times, centuries before Christ.

Recent experiments have shown that such drugs as LSD, psilocybin, and mescaline can produce mystical, visionary experiences of a religious nature of great intensity and reality.* The report of some of these experiments in the book just cited quotes one subject as saying after such an experience under drugs:

> 'I felt a deep union with God . . . I carried my Bible to the altar and tried to preach. The only words I mumbled were peace, peace, peace. I felt I was communicating beyond words' (p. 254 in the chapter headed 'Religious and Mystical Experience').

The use of psychedelic drugs has become so wide-spread, even beyond the United States (where anything is possible!), that some have gone so far as to suggest that the use of drugs, as the basis of religious experience and of the perception of supernatural reality, will form the future world-religion!

Other dead-end streets are also being travelled in this renewed interest in the spiritual and supernatural, in a quest for the spirit which is in no way related to the Christian Gospel. Both white magic in the form of Spiritism or Spiritualism, and black magic in the form of Satanism and the occult, hold many people fascinated; witness the outstanding

* Research has indicated that drugs, and chemical changes in the human body brought about by internal or external stimuli, work on the pineal gland to produce 'super natural' states and visions.

success of William Blatty's best-selling book *The Exorcist* (as well as the film made from this book), and *The Devils*. These cults also substantiate their claims via experience.

What has been submitted above should be adequate to show that the appeal to religious experience as the verification of religious truth can be a very dubious matter indeed. That the Christian faith includes experience is agreed; that it involves the emotions, and not just the intellect and will, is beyond argument. But the insistent questions remain: On what is Christian experience based? How does Christian experience relate to faith?

If the Christian claims to have supernatural signs and experiences, and demonstrations of power, whether speaking in tongues, visions, special revelations, or miraculous healings, he should be aware that there are any number of such phenomena in non-Christian religions and cults. He must be prepared to examine the subjective element in his own experience, no matter how much he believes that the Spirit of God is the great power in his life. But he ought to be able to point to something outside of his own subjectivity as the basis of his faith and hope: the objective Word of God and the promise of the Gospel.

4. The Criteria of Truth

We cannot simply take it for granted that, in the search for the truth concerning the Spirit, charismatics and non-charismatics share the same criteria of truth or the same use of sources. Though both sides in the argument cite the Scriptures (Protestant charismatics also insist on the principle of *Scripture alone*) the questions still remain: a) whether the Scriptures are used and understood in the same way, and b) whether there are not other courts of appeal in the case of charismatics.

1. Much is made in Pentecostal literature of the success story of the charismatic movement. Although there are signs that the original enthusiasm has already died down in some areas of the world, we cannot challenge the fact that the movement of the Spirit' is sweeping the Third World as the so-called 'third force in Christianity'. We can also accept the figures cited, for example, that there are over 30 million charismatics in the world, and that they constitute the most active and virile Christian group in South America and elsewhere. But if success in terms of numerical growth is the test of truth, we would also have to say that the Lord has blessed the Jehovah's Witnesses and other sub-Christian sects. And the biggest success-story of our day is that enjoyed by atheistic materialism, whether in capitalist or communist lands! It is clear that the fundamental issue is God's truth, not documented success.

Non-charismatics, on the other hand, run the danger of arguing on the basis of traditionalism or prejudice against the very term 'Pentecostal'. While the term, for many, has taken on a pejorative sense, one would hope that the whole of Christendom, including the Lutheran Church, is the church of the Holy Spirit, the church of Pentecost. The argument is not over a name!

2. We have noted the dubious nature of **personal experience**, of observable experiential data. Spiritual experiences, such as speaking in strange tongues and faith healing, are in themselves not uniquely Christian phenomena. Even the demonic can produce signs and tongues (this is the implication of Paul's words in 1 Cor. 12:2, where the apostle speaks of the Corinthians' heathen past), and we are entitled to suspect the presence of the demonic in some of the strange 'supernatural' phenomena produced by Spiritualism and the occult.

It will certainly not do to offer a psychological explanation for every subjective religious experience, no matter how much we believe that such things as mass-hysteria and auto-suggestion do play a role in some forms of Pentecostal enthusiasm. But, by the same token, we are not entitled to claim that it is always the Holy Spirit at work where there are claims to supernatural gifts. As we shall see, Paul focuses in 1 Corinthians 12–14 not on the supernatural nature of gifts, but on the goal they are meant to serve: the confession to Christ and the building up of the church. Paul is not concerned with supernatural phenomena as such, but with the question of their use (the 'way' in which they are employed, 1 Cor. 12:31; 13:1). Indeed, Jesus Himself echoes a clear warning against false prophets and deceivers who will appear in the future mouthing the confession to Christ and producing signs and wonders (Matt. 24:24; 7:22–23). As we often see from Jesus' own ministry, the matter of signs is a very dubious area when it comes to proving anything. Only the person who knows the truth of Jesus can understand the truth of a sign, just as only the man who has the Spirit can test the spirits.

Lest we be misunderstood, let it be said again: the issue is not whether there are signs and supernatural events either in the New Testament or today. The question is: How are supernatural events or signs to be interpreted? By themselves they prove nothing.

3. There at least seems to be general agreement on the point that the **history of the church** is not a criterion of truth. It is certainly so that various heretical movements have made special claims on the Spirit, whether early Gnosticism, the Montanist movement of the second century, or the Anabaptist Enthusiasts (*Schwärmer*) against whom Luther had to fight for the truth of the Gospel. But we could also find sufficient evidence in church-history of a quenching of the Spirit and His gifts. The past cannot be used to argue for or against the possibility of a reappearance of charismatic gifts in our own day, even if we maintain that it is God's prerogative to withdraw His gifts in judgment against a church which quenches the Spirit. There can be a poverty of the Spirit which is itself a sign of divine judgment.

4. The only criterion of truth is the **written Word of God**, the Word which was given through the Spirit, and which is used by Him to create and sustain faith. We can look nowhere else for the full truth of the Spirit. It is here that we find both exhortation and warning. 1 Cor. 14:39,40 warns that 'all things should be done decently and in order', but only after Paul has said, 'Earnestly desire to prophesy and do not forbid speaking in tongues'. These words of Paul have their close parallel in 1 Thess. 5:19–21, where he says, 'Do

not quench the Spirit, do not despise prophesying', but goes on to add the important injunction, 'Test everything'. Is it just possible that, in its eagerness to avoid the errors of Corinth, the church has fallen into the opposite error of blocking the path of the Spirit and rejecting His special gifts—all in the name of good order? God gives His gifts in grace, but they can all be abused. The old Latin saying applies: *Abusus non tollit usum*; the possibility of abuse cannot be used to argue against right use. Here both Law and Gospel must be heard.

However, the basic question remains. How is it that evangelical Christians read these passages containing the exhortation and warning of God with respect to the Spirit, and come to different conclusions? Obviously charismatics and non-charismatics read their Bible differently. Recent Anglican studies in this country have correctly highlighted this point (see Paul Barnett and Peter Jensen, *The Quest for Power. Neo-Pentecostals and the New Testament*, ch. 2. 'Reading the Bible', pp. 7–16, and *Both Sides to the Question. Official Enquiry into Neo-Pentecostalism*, pp. 6–9).

Lutherans in approaching their Bible look for Christ, for the Gospel, for the principle and truth of justification by faith as the heart of the New Testament, the key which unlocks the whole truth of Scripture. This means that anything that is claimed as Gospel has to be judged according to the heart of the Gospel, God's free offer of forgiveness in Christ. The real issue with respect to the Spirit and His gifts is not the use of a few orthodox-sounding phrases, but the presentation of the Gospel in consistent Gospel terms. It is not merely a matter of repeating biblical phrases like 'to be baptized with the Spirit', or 'filled with the Spirit', but of understanding what these phrases mean within the context of the whole Gospel of grace.

Although the case is certainly not always clear with neo-Pentecostalism, it can be said that Pentecostalism finally presents us with a new 'gospel'. This claim is vindicated by some Pentecostal denominations which call themselves the Church of the 'Full Gospel' or the 'Four-Square Gospel'. It is reflected in the name of that influential interdenominational organization, the 'Full Gospel Business Men's Fellowship International'. Neo-Pentecostals, while rejecting the legalism of Pentecostals, still often claim the 'plus of the Spirit', something higher and greater after conversion. We have to ask whether this something extra is consistent with the Gospel at all points or whether it detracts from it.

But back to the question of hermeneutics, or the way in which we read our Bible. In what follows we shall speak of Pentecostal exegesis, but many features are also common to the neo-Pentecostal use of Scripture. The trouble with charismatic interpretation of Scripture is not that it is too conservative or literalistic; it is not conservative or literal enough! It insists on preserving exact phrases, such as, 'to be baptized with the Spirit', or 'baptism with the Spirit' (though the noun nowhere appears in the New Testament), without understanding these phrases in consistent Gospel terms. Thus, the gift of the Spirit, which is Gospel, is turned into the necessity to seek the Spirit, which is Law. In their false literalism which absolutizes a genuine biblical phrase, other phrases or passages which have nothing to do with any 'baptism with the Spirit' are pressed into the service of the new 'full gospel'. This can be seen where 1 Cor. 12:13 and Hebrews 6:2 are interpreted in such a way as to teach two baptisms, one with water and one with the Spirit.

The right distinction between Law and Gospel also shows up the falseness of the Pentecostal doctrine of subsequence, which F. D. Bruner has documented for us in his *Theology of the Holy Spirit*. This Pentecostal doctrine maintains that there is a divinely-ordained sequence of events according to which a Christian reaches spiritual maturity and fullness in Christ. First he is reborn by the Word in conversion; then there is the outward sign of this rebirth with water-baptism as the confession of man; then follows total obedience and the baptism of the Spirit. Neo-Pentecostals do not always share this non-sacramental understanding of Baptism, nor do they always make sanctification a prerequisite of Spirit-baptism; nevertheless, they share the view that there is a progression in Christian experience which should follow the pattern or model established in Scripture. They maintain that Scripture has established a divine precedent which should be followed by all Christians.

Even events in Jesus' own life are used to establish this precedent. Just as Jesus was anointed with the Spirit after His baptism in the Jordan, so, they say, all Christians should experience the second blessing of the Spirit after Baptism. The book of Acts is central to the charismatic argument because it is there, so it is claimed, that we find the precedent established in the Early Church.

A Lutheran cannot but suggest that here we have an approach to Scripture that is typical of the Reformed tradition. Claiming to follow biblical precedent, Calvin could set up a new theocracy in Geneva. It is this law of precedent that has allowed some churches to decry the use of any musical instruments in worship apart from the human voice. It is this same approach which legalizes also on matters relating to the administration and celebration of the Sacraments, trying to determine by biblical precedent the kind of bread to be used at the Lord's Supper (leavened or unleavened), or the manner of baptizing (sprinkling or immersion).

Now, one may put up a very good argument for immersion as the **normal** practice in the Early Church. But this does not mean that the manner of administration at that time has established a firm law for all times. If the essence of Baptism as a sacrament of regeneration is Gospel, then the amount of water is not the important thing. If we were to work consistently with biblical precedent we would have to change much in the practical life of the church. We would have to reintroduce the footwashing ceremony (John 13), or hold the Eucharist within the framework of an agape or love-feast as in 1 Corinthians 11. Some might suggest that we should also have all things in common as did the Christians in Acts 2:44,45 and 4:32–37.

Barnett and Jensen rightly warn against the assumption that if the Early Church did something, that is a command from God for us to do it also, thus turning a description (an 'is') into a prescription (an 'ought'). 'The description of a happening in apostolic days is not in itself a command for us to do the same' (*The Quest for Power*, p. 14).

To sum up: The central issue here is not exegetical opinion, or a dispute on the interpretation of a few texts of Scripture, or different forms of piety. We are concerned with the full truth of the full Gospel of free grace, and the individual's certainty about that Gospel and about the life and salvation it offers. Wherever we find an addition to the Gospel which threatens its objective truth, such teaching has to be rejected as another and different gospel coming from a different spirit (Gal. 1:18; 2 Cor. 11:4).

We ought to be especially suspicious of any claim to the Spirit which lives on religious and emotional excitement, where an enthusiasm is let loose which panders to the subjective in man, which allows human faith, obedience, and piety to set the conditions for the coming of the Spirit. We are rightly suspicious where the Spirit is 'used' to prove that which finally cannot be proved, that which remains the object of faith, which simply trusts the promises of God and lives on the 'internal testimony of the Holy Spirit'. For 'faith is the assurance of things hoped for, the conviction of things not seen' (Hebrews 11:1; see also John 20:29). 'We walk by faith, not by sight' (2 Cor: 5:7)!

The central questions which we will keep in mind now as we begin our biblical study are the following:

1. How is the presence and word of the Spirit manifested? Must His presence be demonstrated with supernatural signs?
2. Is there a separate 'baptism of the Spirit', apart from Baptism, without which a man has not received the Spirit, and without which he cannot reach full spiritual maturity?
3. To what is the promise of the Spirit bound: to the Word whether read and preached and acted (Sacrament), or to some experience apart from the Word of God? How is the Spirit received according to the New Testament?
4. What is the specific place of Pentecost in the Early Church? In what sense is it a unique event, and in what sense is it a promise of things to come?
5. Are the gifts of the Spirit available to Christians today? What is their meaning and place in the life and ministry of the church? What is the difference between the 'gifts' and the 'fruit' of the Spirit?

Chapter III

THE MYSTERY OF DIVINE CREATIVE POWER

1. The Spirit of Creation and Revelation

The controversy over the Spirit and His gifts, as well as the so called 'baptism of the Spirit', involves the interpretation of certain key New Testament passages, in the Gospels, in Acts, and especially in 1 Corinthians 12–14.

We could immediately take up the question of this 'baptism', and the meaning of charismatic gifts such as tongues. But the danger in that approach is that certain individual features of the New Testament teaching on the Spirit might be treated without keeping in focus the whole biblical picture of the Spirit and His work within the plan of God. Again, a systematic treatment which draws on isolated texts from all over the New Testament runs the danger of losing sight of those special accents which belong to the various New Testament writings, and which are linked to the historical settings in which they were written.

However, before taking up our New Testament study, a brief look at the Spirit in the Old Testament is in place. As indicated earlier, the New Testament writers did not offer a full and explicit witness to the Spirit because they did not have to argue for the reality of spirit in contrast to matter, or for the Holy Spirit in contradistinction to the spirit of man. In addition, they could presuppose the Old Testament references to God's Spirit and His power.

From the first to the last pages of the Bible, the Holy Spirit remains surrounded by mystery—even though he is the Comforter and is known to every believer. He who moved over and above the face of the waters at the dawn of the world (Gen. 1:2) moves over and above the spirit of man. He cannot be dictated to or manipulated by man; He continues to move and work as He wills (John 3:8).

The revelation of His divine personhood remains largely hidden in the Old Testament. Indeed, while we think of 'spirit' in masculine terms, the Old Testament Hebrew word *ruach* is feminine in gender (the Greek *pneuma* is neuter, while the Latin *spiritus* is masculine). The Old Testament speaks of 'the Spirit of God', or God Himself speaks of 'My Spirit', but there is as yet no full revelation of the personhood of the Spirit within the Trinity. Without the New Testament witness we might be justified in thinking of the Spirit merely as the power of God, as a creative, life-giving principle, as that which marks God as God in contrast to His created visible world. Only occasionally do we find a slight suggestion that the Spirit may be spoken of as a person over against God (see 1 Kings 22:19–24; 2 Chron. 18:20–23; Ezek. 37:9).

Just as His person is shrouded in mystery, so also His work remains mysterious, as part of the inscrutable and unpredictable will of God. Nevertheless, His work is there to be seen by the eye of faith. He is the **dynamic,**

creative breath of God by which all things came into being. 'By the word of the Lord the heavens were made, and all their host by the breath (*ruach*) of his mouth' (Ps. 33:6). He it is in whom all living creatures have life. It is the breath or Spirit of God that was breathed into man to make him a living soul (the Hebrew word *ruach*, like the Greek *pneuma*, means either wind, breath, or spirit), but it is the same breath which gives all creatures life (Gen. 2:7; 6:17). The Spirit also participates in the divine work of preservation, for without Him life would cease to exist (Gen. 6:3). Thus, that suffering saint Job confesses: 'The spirit of God has made me, and the breath of the Almighty gives me life' (Job 33:4), 'If he should take back his spirit to himself, and gather to himself his breath, all flesh would perish together, and man would return to dust' (Job 34:14,15; see also 27:3 and Ps. 104:29,30).

Furthermore, He is the **origin of God's special gifts**. It is the Spirit who enables individual people to carry out His special tasks. We can certainly speak of charismatic gifts and of charismatic leaders already in the Old Testament. We see this divine power at work supplying wisdom and leadership qualities in such men as Moses and Aaron (Num. 11:17–29). The Spirit is even spoken of in quantitative terms, as a power that can be transferred from one carrier to another. Thus God took 'some of the spirit' that was upon Moses and put it on the seventy elders chosen to assist Moses in ruling over Israel. An external sign, the gift of prophecy, even confirmed this transferral of power, even though the certifying gift was not a lasting one (v. 25). Joshua was also commissioned as Israel's new leader as one 'in whom is the spirit' (Num. 27:18).

But the most famous charismatic leaders in Israel's history were those men given the title of Judges. The title did not indicate a judicial role so much as a God-given call to be a deliverer of Israel. Judges 2:6–3:5 gives the theological thrust of the whole book and the key to an understanding of this period of Israel's history. Israel repeatedly neglected the worship of God and served the heathen Baals, the fertility gods of Canaan. In answer, God called up various surrounding nations to harry and punish His disobedient people. After their repenting and crying to God for deliverance from their enemies, God called a succession of 'deliverers' who defeated the enemy. In each case the Judge was equipped with a gift of the Spirit. 'The Spirit of the Lord came upon him' is something like a programmatic opening to the reference to each of them—Othniel (Judges 10); Gideon (6:34); Jephthah (11:29); Samson (13:25). That these charismatic gifts were not obviously supernatural gifts, and had nothing to do with special spiritual qualities, is best illustrated from the last and most famous Judge, Samson. His gifts were cunning, and unusual physical strength (that the latter was given by the Spirit is quite clear in 14:6,19 and 15:14).

The same Spirit came on Saul and David at their anointing for kingship (1 Sam. 11:6; 16:13). We see men suddenly gifted with a power which cannot be explained in simple human terms. Men were transformed into great leaders with wonderful qualities of leadership, wisdom, and courage. The transformation in the case of Saul was so great that it can be said that he was 'turned into another man' (1 Sam. 10:6–13, and especially v. 6). Here, certainly, the special gift of the Spirit was accompanied by what we must call a supernatural sign, for Saul prophesied with the prophets whom he met. Although the prophetic gift was later given to Saul on one more occasion, raising the famous question, 'Is Saul also among the prophets?' (19:24), this gift was not a permanent possession as it was with the prophets.

The mysterious **revealing power** of the Spirit which man cannot withstand, which can even gain control of a man against his will (as seen in the above case of Saul and his servants in 1 Sam. 19:18–24), is the same power which moved the Old Testament prophets to become spokesmen of God, using speech that was anything but ecstatic or supernatural. The word 'prophet' has, in most languages, become synonymous with '*foreteller*'. But the Greek word behind 'prophet' designates him rather as a '*for-teller*' or '*forth-teller*'. Certainly, less than half the prophetic oracles of the Old Testament are predictions about the future. Their message contains oracles of doom and of judgment, calls to repentance, recollections of God's mercy in the past, assurances of His presence in the present, as well as prophetic oracles relating to judgment and salvation in the future.

In certain cases the prophet was the recipient of revelation via dreams and visions (Ezek. 11:24; 37:1). As God's spokesman, as a 'man of the Spirit', his possession of the Spirit could be marked by ecstatic states which led men to call him mad (Hosea 9:7). However, ecstatic foretelling of the future was not the characteristic mark of the Old Testament prophet. The prophet, like the king, was simply one who was anointed with 'the Spirit of the Lord God' (Isa. 61:1) or 'filled with power, with the Spirit of the Lord' (Micah 3:8). The Spirit set the prophet on his feet (Ezek. 2:2); the prophet spoke Yahweh's words as sent by His Spirit (Zech. 7:12). But the possession of the Spirit and of the prophetic gift was not always certifiable. The question arose from time to time: Which prophet is speaking the truth? Who is the true prophet? What is the difference between a true prophet who does speak the message of the Lord, and a mad man or a prophet with a lying spirit (see the confrontation between Jeremiah and Hananiah in Jer. 28)? The test of prophecy enunciated in Deut. 18:21,22 and Jer. 28:9 (only the future will tell whether a prophet has been a genuine spokesman of the Lord) did not exactly make it easy for contemporaries to test the spirits!

If frenzy and ecstasy were the mark of the true prophet, there would be little to distinguish him from the prophet of Baal, dancing about and gashing himself with a knife (1 Kings 18:28). It was not any acting as a medium which set apart the Old Testament prophet as unique from the prophets of Canaan, Egypt, or Mesopotamia, but rather the Spirit who moved him, and the actual message he spoke. In the case of some prophets, their message was very much marked by their own personality. This was certainly the case with Jeremiah, who, though a man of the Spirit, often struggled to carry out his call to speak the word of judgment on God's people of which he was a member. When Amos said to Amaziah, the priest of Bethel: 'I am no prophet, nor a prophet's son [literally, '*one of the sons of the prophets*']; but I am a herdsman, and a dresser of sycamore trees' (Amos 7:14), he spoke on behalf of the whole band of Old Testament prophets. They were not members of priestly schools, or officials of the cult; they remained voices crying out in the wilderness, certified only by their call to repentance, faith, and hope. Even as men of the Spirit, their only power was the Word of Yahweh which came to them from the Spirit.

2. The Spirit and the New Creation

Already in the Old Testament, the Spirit is known and depicted as the possession of every person who trusts in the Lord, the preserver of that righteousness which means a right relationship with God. The psalmist not only knew of the breath of life that sustained his physical existence, that kept him from collapsing into a pile of dust (Job 34:14,15), he also knew of the Spirit of renewal and holiness. And so he prayed, 'Take not thy holy Spirit from me', and asked for a new heart and a new spirit (Ps. 51:10–12); he pleaded that God would teach him His will, that he might be led by God's good Spirit (Ps. 143:10). There was no trace here of the later Hellenistic idea that man's spirit by nature is potentially divine; the psalmist knows man to be fallible and corruptible flesh. Man can only be 'spiritual' by the power of the divine, life-giving Spirit of God. The Spirit is God's to give in grace, and His to take away in judgment—as in the case of Saul (1 Sam. 16:14).

The Old Testament people of God certainly knew and confessed the Gospel of the Spirit as they knew it. They knew of the gracious Spirit's work in creation and preservation, in the history of God's great saving acts (Neh. 9:20; Hag. 2:5), and in the life of God's saints individually. The Spirit was the assurance of God's saving presence among His people. Strange to say, the psalmist could even find grace in the fact that he, mere lowly man, could never flee or escape from the Spirit of God. 'Whither shall I go from thy Spirit?' he asked, and knew very well that the Spirit, as God Himself, would follow him into heaven or Sheol, to far distant lands, or into the darkness of night: 'Even there thy hand shall lead me, and thy right hand shall hold me' (Ps. 139:7–12).

Despite all this, the Gospel of the Spirit only began to unfold more fully as the prophets promised the creation of a new people of God out of the remnant of the judged and exiled Israel. It is more than a little fascinating to note how the Spirit began to figure very prominently as soon as the day of hope loomed large on the horizon. The future day of restoration would not come 'until the Spirit is poured . . . from on high' (Isa. 32:15). Israel continued to be like dry thirsty ground, but the great promise was given through the prophet Isaiah, 'I will pour my Spirit upon your descendants, and my blessing on your offspring' (44:3). In this great day, Israel would once more be like a fruitful field, showing the fruits of righteousness.

Without doubt, the most graphic picture of this renewing activity of the Spirit in Israel's future history is that found in the famous vision of Ezekiel (Ezek. 37). The prophet sees a valley covered with very dry bones. When asked 'Can these bones live?', he answers God with a very diplomatic 'You are the only one who knows the answer to that, God'! At the word of the prophet, the Spirit or breath of God is summoned, thereupon reassembling the bones into skeletons, and then corpses, and finally breathing life into them to form a huge host of people. The message is clear. Without God's life-giving Spirit, Israel was as good as dead in her Babylonian Captivity. But God who first breathed His Spirit into Adam would again create for Himself a new people, where now there was only hopelessness and death. And so Ezekiel became the prophet of the Gospel of the Spirit. Through him there came the magnificent promise:

> 'I will give them one heart, and put a new spirit within them; I will take the stony heart out of their flesh, and give them a heart of flesh' (Ezek. 11:19; cf. 18:31).

An even more graphic picture of the future transformation followed:

> 'I will take you from the nations . . . and bring you into your own land. I will sprinkle clean water upon you, and you shall be clean from all your uncleanness . . . . A new heart I will give you, and a new spirit I will put within you; and I will take out of your flesh the heart of stone and give you a heart of flesh. And I will put my spirit within you and cause you to walk in my statutes . . . and you shall be my people, and I will be your God.' (Ezek. 36:24–28).

The very last statement of Ezekiel before his vision of the new temple and cult in Jerusalem was, 'I will not hide my face any more from them, when I pour out my Spirit upon the house of Israel, says the Lord God' (39:29). This was the promise that was again taken up by Joel:

> 'I will pour out my spirit on all flesh; your sons and daughters shall prophesy, your old men shall dream dreams, and your young men shall see visions. Even upon the menservants and maid servants in those days, I will pour out my spirit.' (Joel 2:28,29).

Two observations will serve to highlight the importance of this last group of prophecies in their relationship to the New Testament.

First, it is the Joel prophecy which Peter cites in his Pentecost sermon in Acts 2. But it is also interesting to note that in Ezekiel and Joel the Spirit is spoken of in 'fluid' terms. He will be 'poured out'. His renewing work will be a washing or sprinkling with clean water. Water, as a basic life-giving element, is a natural image for the Spirit; and it is this image that reappears in the New Testament at various points, not only in the explicit image in John 7:37–39, but also in such phrases as 'to be baptized in the Holy Spirit', or 'to be filled with the Spirit', as well as 'to pour out the Spirit'.

Secondly, the Joel prophecy goes beyond the prophecies of Ezekiel in several ways. Every member of Israel, from master to servant, from male to female, would be filled with the Spirit of God. No longer would His power rest only on certain chosen servants of God, whether prophets, priests, or kings. Again, when the Spirit is poured out, His presence would be certified by those signs which normally characterized the role of those specially-chosen spokesmen of God, the prophets. In the future age of renewal, all men would know the will of God, for God would be fully revealed to the whole house of Israel.

Isaiah, Ezekiel, and Joel were, thus, united in their message of an age of renewal for God's people, an age that would be marked by the common possession of the Spirit by **all**, so that **all** would know God's will and be empowered to do it. If this were to come about, it would be 'not by [man's] might, nor by [man's] power, but by my Spirit, says the Lord of hosts' (Zech. 4:6).

However, the picture of the great future that lay in store for Israel did not stop at this. Even if there were only few hints at this, the age of the Spirit would also be the age of the Messiah. Isaiah gives the promise concerning the branch of Jesse on whom

> 'the Spirit of the Lord shall rest . . . , the spirit of wisdom and understanding, the spirit of counsel and might, the spirit of knowledge and fear of the Lord' (Isa. 11:2).

It could, of course, be argued that Spirit at the beginning of the above passage could also be written 'spirit'–with a small *s*. But that Isaiah is referring to nothing less than the Spirit of God Himself is suggested by another passage which speaks of the Suffering Servant. Israel is, indeed, God's servant, as are also the prophet and other divinely-appointed agents of God's will. But there emerges in Isaiah that lone figure who suffers for the sins of his people (Isa. 53), and to whom that prophetic word also applies:

> 'Behold my servant, whom I uphold, my chosen, in whom my soul delights;
> I have put my Spirit upon him, he will bring forth justice to the nations' (Isa. 42:1; cf. also Zech. 12:10).

The quest for the Spirit of God ends in the Old Testament not with fulfilment, but with a promise. The era of the Spirit is still around the corner. But it is coming; there is nothing surer than this!

Chapter IV

THE SPIRIT-FILLED MESSIAH

As soon as we begin to read the Gospel accounts, the Old Testament prophecies begin to come alive. But it is not immediately a new Spirit-filled people that appears on the stage of history; rather, it is the Representative Man, the New Israel and the New Adam in one person.

Every mention of the Holy Spirit points to Christ. It is through His divine, creative power that the Messiah is born of a virgin (Matt. 1:18–29; Luke 1:35). This event is not a biological oddity, but a divine miracle inaugurating the age of the Spirit-filled Messiah. The incarnation of God's Son by the power of the Spirit marks the beginning of a new age. John the Baptist saw this so clearly that he could characterize the work of the 'coming one' as a 'baptizing with the Holy Spirit'.

1. The Promise of the Baptizer

It is at this point that we must begin our dialogue with charismatic theology, for this saying of John reported in Matt. 3:11, Mark 1:8, and Luke 3:16 (as well as the related passages in John 1:33, Acts 1:5 and 11:16) is a key-passage in the Pentecostal argument for a second baptism of the Spirit which comes after, and is more important than, water-baptism. Neo-Pentecostals, while not always using the passage in the same way to deprecate water-baptism, still use this saying of John to argue for a special baptism of the Spirit as a second experience of grace.

Whatever the origins of John's baptism (whether Old Testament priestly ritual washings for purification, or prophetical symbolical acts as we find them especially in the books of Jeremiah and Ezekiel, or even proselyte baptism in first-century Judaism), it is surely clear that John's baptism is not a sacrament in the full Christian sense. The exact historical connection between the baptism of John and that performed by Jesus' own disciples (see John 3:22,23 and 4:1–3) is not at all clear.

What is clear is the great contrast contained in John's words. This is stressed in all three Synoptic Gospels by the emphatic position of 'he' (*autos*), and in Mark by the addition of the little particle meaning 'but' (*de*). 'I have baptized you with water; **but he** will baptize you with the Holy Spirit' (1:8). Matthew and Luke add at the end of this sentence the words 'and with fire'. We need not debate at length the two forms of the saying; suffice it to say that the Spirit and fire belong naturally together as a pair, not only because of the tongues of fire at Pentecost (Acts 2; see also the phrase 'do not quench the Spirit' in 1 Thess. 5:19 which invokes the image of putting out a fire!), but because they together form a couplet suggesting divine activity in terms of judgment and renewal. That the Spirit means renewal hardly needs further demonstration after our comments on the Old

Testament above, and Matt. 3:10–12 illustrates clearly enough the theme of judgment implied with fire (the same picture is found in 1 Cor. 3:13–15 where fire is a purifying and refining agent).

John thus promises the coming of the Messianic age which will bring both purification and renewal. The future baptism is one, not two baptisms (the one preposition 'with' governs both nouns); it offers no alternative to John's baptism, but will supersede it. But this raises the question: How far does the contrast extend? Charismatics often see Christian Baptism merely as an extension of John's baptism. To them, the real, the important, the characteristic baptism of the new age is the baptism of the Spirit, without water. The Spirit is even spoken of as the new element, in contrast to water. Thus, it is maintained: in Christian Baptism, the church baptizes; in 'Spirit-baptism', it is Christ who baptizes!

Certainly, **mere water** is contrasted with the Spirit, but it is going too far to say that the future baptism of the Spirit has nothing to do with water. Here great caution is necessary. We cannot categorically say that John is referring to the later Christian sacrament of Baptism; he could hardly look beyond Pentecost and see the precise way in which the Spirit would be given to all men. The text simply emphasizes that the characteristic gift of the Messiah is the Spirit. However, it is clear from both Luke (Acts 2:38,39) and Paul (1 Cor. 12:13) that the Early Church did not make a separation between Baptism and the pouring out of the Spirit.

Thus the **how** of the Spirit's coming is not the point of John's prophecy. But for the moment we can, at least, say the following:

1. In his conversation with Nicodemus, Jesus points to the necessity of being 'born of water and the Spirit' (John 3:5). Here again water and Spirit are hardly contrasted (once again the one preposition 'of' (*ek*) governs the two nouns). While it has been argued from time to time that 'water' here refers to John's baptism, this can hardly be the case. There is, surely, not the slightest hint that John's baptism was a washing of renewal (in John's Gospel the baptism of John is not even the most important feature of his ministry; he is, rather, the first great witness to Christ), whereas we do find in Titus 3:5 a reference to the 'washing of regeneration and renewal in the Holy Spirit' which is obviously a clear reference to Christian Baptism.

2. The phrase 'to be baptized with the Holy Spirit' implies a metaphorical use of the term 'baptize', and need not in itself point to a rite involving washing. We find another metaphorical use of the verb in Mark 10:38,39 and Luke 12:50, where the 'baptism' of Jesus is His being immersed in His passion. Although the metaphor of the Spirit as water (seen already in certain Old Testament passages) is still carried on in the New Testament with certain phrases (e.g. the 'pouring out' of the Spirit), the metaphor of baptism itself became less appropriate in time. The reason for this is clear. The phrase 'to be baptized with the Spirit' occurs only once apart from the references to this saying of John in the Gospels and Acts, and where it does occur (1 Cor. 12:13) it is clearly used of the Sacrament of Baptism which

imparts the Spirit. Thus, for the Early Church there was, in the proper sense, only 'one baptism', as the creed of Eph. 4:4–6 confesses.

3. In view of the above, John's words do not contrast baptism as such, but only the essence—water and Spirit. F. D. Bruner rightly points out that the words, indeed, not only include a contrast; they also imply a combination, for baptism is the thing common to both parts of his saying. 'Baptism in the Spirit meant what the words say, **baptism**, and that, namely, in the **Spirit**' (*A Theology of the Holy Spirit*, p. 219). Furthermore, it is equally clear that baptism in the Spirit is not distinct from entry into the kingdom of God, but constitutes the very way into it. It is just as the Spirit-filled and Spirit-promising Messiah that Jesus preached the kingdom of God. Any charismatic argument which argues that there is first an entry into the kingdom, and then an additional experience in the form of a Spirit-baptism (quite apart from the Spirit-worked entry into the kingdom), finds no support in John the Baptist's famous saying.

Of course, the meaning of this saying cannot be decided by an examination of the Gospel accounts alone. Acts 1:5 and 11:16 show that this promise or prophecy of John was fulfilled at Pentecost and on subsequent occasions in Acts. But we shall turn to these passages later.

2. The Baptism and Temptation of Jesus

Before He began His public ministry, the Messiah was Himself 'anointed . . . with the Holy Spirit and with power' (Acts 10:38). As Jesus came up from the waters of the Jordan River after His baptism, the Spirit descended upon Him in the likeness of a dove, and a heavenly voice proclaimed Jesus as 'my beloved Son' (Matt. 3:16,17; Mark 1:10; Luke 3:21,22). In John's Gospel the account of the actual baptism is missing, but the descent of the Spirit and His 'remaining' on Jesus is recalled by the Baptist (John 1:32). John, therefore, like the others, pictures Jesus as the Spirit-filled Messiah and Son of God.

This scene also plays an important role in Pentecostal literature, and (although to a lesser extent) in neo-Pentecostal arguments for a special baptism of the Spirit. Their argument, in brief, is as follows: Just as Jesus first experienced a supernatural birth through the Spirit (Matt. 1:18–20; Luke 1:35), then obeyed the Father perfectly by submitting to John's water-baptism (the reference is to Jesus 'fulfilling all righteousness' in Matt. 3:15), and only then underwent the second experience of the Spirit, so also all Christians after their rebirth by the Spirit (conversion) and its accompanying sign, water-baptism, should experience the second blessing of the Spirit-baptism as the fruit of faith and obedience. Just as Jesus was anointed at the Jordan for His mission, so all Christians should pray for, and expect to receive, the 'promise of the Father' to equip them for service and a ministry of witness. (The above argument is naturally different in the case of those charismatics who, unlike Pentecostals, still see Baptism as a sacrament of regeneration, and refuse to accept the Pentecostal stress on holiness as a prerequisite for the 'second blessing'.)

The argument at first sight seems very strong, especially in view of Acts 10:38. But this understanding of Jesus' baptism not only says too much; it also says too little! As James D. G. Dunn points out in his careful study of this episode in his book, *Baptism in the Holy Spirit*, the attempt to turn Jesus' baptism into a precedent or pattern for Christian experience fails to see **the unique** character of this event within the story of salvation. Dunn rightly speaks of its 'pivotal' importance. Though Jesus' baptism does, indeed, have much to do with baptism of water and the Spirit, 'it cannot be used as an exact precedent which establishes conditions to be met by later Christians; it does not establish a set order of Christian experience. In passing, we should note that while the Early Church, and later Luther himself, did find in this event the beginnings of Christian Baptism as a sacrament of grace, that Sacrament is first explicitly referred to in Matt. 28:19. Baptism, as it is known in Acts and in Paul's letters, is clearly a sacrament which presupposes Christ's death and resurrection, as well as the outpouring of the Spirit at Pentecost (Acts 2:32,33; Rom. 6:1–4).

Jesus' baptism is not simply one stage in a series of stages in Jesus' spiritual life, but a stage in salvation-history. It is part of the unfolding of the Gospel itself, since its real point is the proclamation, even acclamation, of the Messiah 'from above'. The event is, thus, only properly seen when viewed as the **inauguration of the Messianic age**.

The uniqueness of the event is seen from three features alone—the rending of the heavens (an apocalyptic motif), the dove, and the heavenly voice. Just as the Greek word *anōthen* ('from above') is used in John 3:7 and James 1:17 to describe the origin of God's good gifts, especially the great gift of the Spirit, so here we have a divine invasion of grace into history with the tearing-open of the heavens, and the voice from heaven which certifies that the Messiah has arrived. The coming of the Spirit on Jesus is unique, because His person is unique.

It will still be argued by charismatics that Jesus' reception of the Spirit is the important thing. But Dunn again puts the matter in correct perspective when he writes:

> 'The coming of the Spirit on Jesus effects not so much a change in Jesus, his person or his status, as the beginning of a new stage of salvation-history. The thought is not so much of Jesus becoming what he was not before, but of Jesus entering where he was not before, a new epoch in God's plan of redemption.' (*Baptism in the Holy Spirit*, p. 28).

Both Matthew and Luke make it clear that Jesus is Messiah and Son of God from His birth, even before His baptism (see, for example, Luke 1:35,43,76; 2:11,26,49). There is, of course, a sense in which He enters His Messianic role at the Jordan, since it is here that He is 'anointed with power' and is proclaimed as the Son. We again recall Peter's words in Acts 10:38, and also note how Luke 4:18 takes up Isa. 61:1,2. Likewise, even though Jesus is the eternal Son of God (John 1), there is also a sense in which He becomes the Son only after His glorification. Rom. 1:3 confesses Jesus the Lord who was 'designated Son of God in power according to the Spirit of holiness [a Jewish expression for 'Holy Spirit'] by his resurrection from the dead'. The Spirit is the power behind His birth, His royal acclamation after His baptism, and His glorification. Certainly, there are various Christologies in the New Testament; the truth is too rich to be compressed into one formula. There was one which stressed His pre-existence as the Son in all eternity, one which spoke of His adoption by the Father at His baptism (using the royal-adoption formula of Ps. 2:7), and one which spoke of Him being raised to this position after His glorification (this ascension Christology is characteristic of Luke's theology in Acts; cf. 2:36 and 13:33). What we have in all three cases are not stages in Jesus' personal religious experience, but a movement towards the grand climax, the universal confession of Jesus Christ as Lord, Son, and Messiah (see also how the hymns to Christ in Phil. 2:5–11 and Hebrews 1:3,4 climax in the bestowal of 'the name'!). The church learned to confess that Jesus had always been the Son, that He was Messiah in God's eternal plan long before His baptism and anointing with the Spirit. The gift of the Spirit added nothing to His person as such, but certified Him as the one who could now enter His Messianic role with the power of God resting on Him.

In that role He was completely unique. There can be no suggestion of His setting a pattern of progress in the spiritual life of every believer. This is not the *imitatio Christi* that the New Testament speaks about!

The uniqueness of this event is established further by the setting of the story in the Gospel narratives, as well as other interpretative features. The descent of the Spirit stamps Jesus not only as the Messiah, but also as the Israel of the last times, and the Second Adam, the perfect obedient man. The king and the servant-figure to whom Ps. 2:7 and Isa. 42:1 first apply the terms 'Son' and 'beloved' are representative figures. In addition, Israel is itself called God's son in the Old Testament (for example, Ex. 4:22 speaks of Israel as God's 'first-born son'). Here in Jesus we find the perfect Israel of the end-time, the final Adam, the King Himself!

These features come out most clearly in the **temptation narratives** which immediately follow the Jordan scene. At His temptation the Sonship of Jesus is placed on trial by Satan. And it is not by chance that the Spirit figures prominently in this account also (see Mark 1:12 and Matt. 4:1, but especially Luke 4:1 and 14). Jesus is 'led by the Spirit into the wilderness' for this testing: Mark puts it even more forcefully when he writes that Jesus is driven out into the wilderness by the Spirit! The Spirit directs Jesus on His mission from the moment it begins; indeed, it would seem that the test itself is 'set up' by the Spirit. The key-question of Satan points back to the heavenly voice of Jesus' baptism, for it runs: 'If you are the Son of God, then . . .'

Jesus stands the test, so that the demons have to recognize His Sonship immediately the clash with the kingdom of Satan begins (Luke 4:41). But, as we suggested, He proves to be more than Son of God. In contrast to Israel who were disobedient in the wilderness during the Exodus-wanderings, He shows Himself to be the true obedient Israel. The story of the temptation recalls the wilderness-wandering in two ways. Not only was Jesus out in the lonely place for 40 days and nights, just as Israel was in the wilderness for 40 years; Jesus also answers His tempter with texts taken from Deut. 6–8.

As various commentators have shown, the emphasis in Luke is rather on Jesus as the final obedient Adam. The contrast between the two Adams is known from Paul's writings (Rom. 5:12–21; 1 Cor. 15:45–50; Phil. 2:6–8). The Adam-parallel, or contrast, is suggested in Luke's Gospel by the placing of the family tree of Jesus between the accounts of His baptism and temptation. And whereas Matthew traces Jesus' lineage back to Abraham, Luke traces it back to Adam. The last words before the temptation-story are, significantly, 'Adam, the son of God' (Luke 3:37)!

What are the consequences of all this for our study? If we have belaboured the last few points somewhat, it has been done with the aim of establishing a method of approach to the Gospel narrative which goes beyond taking it as biblical precedent. We can now state some conclusions:

1. The obedience of Jesus was not a precondition for His anointing with the Spirit. Rather, the test of obedience and Sonship followed the anointing with the Spirit at His baptism. The saying about Jesus having to fulfil all righteousness (Matt. 3:15) dare not be taken as establishing the necessity of fulfilling certain moral obligations before the Spirit can be given or received. There is not even any precise mention of Jesus having requested the Spirit, not even in Luke 3:21. Nor does He meet any prior preconditions for acceptance. Here, as always, the Spirit is the gracious gift from heaven.

2. The reception of the Spirit certainly meant the gift of power. How this power can be added to Him who is the God-man and, in the confession of the church, one with the Father and Spirit in all eternity, remains a mystery. However, the clear stress in the narrative of Jesus' baptism and temptation is on the Christological function and focus of the Spirit. The Spirit always points beyond or away from Himself to Christ. It is in keeping with the whole picture of the work of the Spirit that His coming always climaxes in the confession to Christ. Here the Father confesses His own Son! The Spirit comes not to glorify Himself, or to be felt and experienced for Himself, but to glorify the Son. That this point is seen and stressed by many charismatics must also be acknowledged; see the testimony in Larry Christenson's *Speaking in Tongues*: 'Brethren, it's Jesus. It's Jesus. The Holy Spirit comes to glorify Jesus' (p. 59).

3. Bruner has reminded us that the temptation-narrative has further significance for our discussion in that it implies a rejection of any certification of the Spirit's power in terms of wonders and miracles. Jesus refused to prove His Sonship and possession of the Spirit with a display of power. The desire for spiritual power is

perhaps the most refined of temptations. For it often leads either to the manipulating of God (what we might call white magic), or to doubt in God with whom alone is true power. Where the quest for power becomes paramount, it may often lead to power, but not exercised in the service of God (Matt. 4:10; Luke 4:8; see Matt. 7:22,23). The seeking of signs to prove one's own power is the primal temptation, and reflects the desire for evidence instead of faithful submission to the word of the Father.

4. One point must be granted to charismatic interpretation. We cannot argue from the story of Jesus' baptism and temptation that baptism with water is automatically always a baptism with the Spirit. It also belongs to the uniqueness of the Jordan-event that its climax is not Jesus' baptism but His anointing with the Spirit. But, by the same token, the accounts cannot be used in an attempt to prove that water-baptism and Spirit-baptism are always separate, distinct events, which can be isolated from each other. To be quite precise, of course, the texts do not even say that Jesus was 'baptized with the Spirit'. The choice of the word 'anointed' again points to the uniqueness of the event. Here is the Spirit-filled Messiah! And Messiah means 'the Anointed'.

3. The Promise of the Spirit

No sooner did Jesus step into public view than His claim to the Spirit was voiced loud and clear. His very first sermon proclaimed, in the words of Isa. 61:1,2: 'The Spirit of the Lord God is upon me, because the Lord has anointed me to bring good tidings to the afflicted' (Luke 4:18,19). He publicly claimed to be the Servant of Isa. 42:1 on whom God has placed His Spirit (Matt. 12:18).

Secondly, Jesus not only **spoke** with power as the Prophet of God, He also **acted** with power (*exousia*). Mark and Luke, hardly by accident, show that Jesus' first public action involved a clash with the demonic world (Mark 1:21–28; Luke 4:31–37; see also Matt. 4:24). The Spirit-filled Messiah and Prophet not only preached the kingdom of God; He also attacked the other spiritual realm, the kingdom of Satan.

And yet a quick look at the occurrence of the word 'Spirit' in the **Synoptic Gospels** causes some surprise. The word occurs some 11 times in Matthew's Gospel, only 6 times in Mark, and some 18 in Luke. Compare this with over 200 occurrences in John's Gospel, over 50 in Acts, and over 30 in both Romans and 1 Corinthians. We cannot explain this phenomenon simply by saying that the Gospels proclaim Jesus, whereas Acts and Paul's Letters give us the story of the Spirit.

We have seen that there are four blocks of material at the beginning of the Synoptic Gospels where the Spirit plays a key-role in the ushering in of the Kingdom (Jesus' birth, the ministry and prophecy of John the Baptist, Jesus' baptism, and His temptation). But once Jesus had stepped into the middle of the stage, the Spirit is hardly mentioned. This feature, far from suggesting that Jesus replaces the Spirit, says just the opposite: The work of the Spirit in and through Jesus had been established clearly enough to require only a few explicit references to the Spirit's work. Matt. 12:28 shows how the work of the Spirit and Jesus are one. 'If it is by the Spirit of God that I cast out demons, then the kingdom of God has come upon you.' It is as the one who fully possessed God's Spirit that Jesus was led to a prophetic and joyful view of God's gracious revealing of Himself, and the saving efficacy of that revelation (Luke 10:21). As one who had the Spirit, Jesus fully knew the will of the Father.

There is, in a sense, no new theology of the Spirit in the Gospels. We find references to His work in inspiring men in the Old Testament (Mark 12:36; Matt. 22:43). And there is, as has often been pointed out, a decidedly Old Testament flavour about the role of the Spirit in the preparatory history of Luke's Gospel. The Baptizer is filled with the Spirit already in his mother's womb; his parents also are filled with the Spirit to utter prophetic words (Luke 1:15,17,41,67). Likewise the aged Simeon is under the Spirit's special direction.

There is in Luke's infancy-narratives a new activity of the Spirit after centuries of silence. And this activity continues in the ministry of Jesus. But John's Gospel reminds us that Jesus not only **spoke** the Word of God. He **was** the Word incarnate. Jesus was not gifted merely with moments of charismatic power. As the Word in person He **was** the power of God, as the one on whom God had poured out His Spirit without measure (John 3:34). And so, despite the few references to the Spirit, the earthly ministry of Jesus, His death and resurrection, place before men the final unlimited action of the Spirit of God.

C. K. Barrett, in *The Holy Spirit and the Gospel Tradition*, has suggested other good reasons for the comparatively few references to the Spirit during the ministry of Jesus. Jesus always acted under the necessity of divine constraint ('I **must** do the will of him who sent me') as the secret Messiah. Thus 'to have claimed a pre-eminent measure of the Spirit would have been to make an open confession of Messiahship'. Rather, 'lack of glory and a cup of suffering were his Messianic vocation' (p. 158). Again:

> 'Jesus returns from victory [over Satan in the desert] with the conviction that the way of God's Chosen is the way of humility and weakness, and from that time references to the Spirit are very few indeed. Even his miracles, though it is not hard to detect the marks of 'pneumatic' thaumaturgy upon them, are not compelling signs, but are of significance and value only to the elect, and not to those who are without.' (p. 159).

That which characterizes the Spirit in the New Testament is not a new theology of His person, but a new operation, a new promise, a new reference to God's saving work in Christ. The Spirit never occupies an independent position alongside Jesus. Nor does Luke, who shows a special interest in the Spirit in his twin-work of Gospel and Acts, speak of an age of Jesus in contrast to an age of the Spirit. The latter always remains the 'Spirit of God' as much as He remains the 'Spirit of Jesus'.

This also becomes clear as Jesus looks, and points His disciples, beyond the present to the future where they will not only need, but have, the Spirit.

In passing we should also note that the sayings of Jesus about blasphemy against the Spirit are placed in a Christological context. Matt. 12:31,32, for example, is preceded by v. 30: 'He who is not with me is against me . . .'. This point is possibly even clearer in Luke 12:9,10, verses which link the sin against the Spirit with the denial of Christ Himself! (see also Mark 3:28–30).

The continuation of this last Lucan passage climaxes in the promise of the Spirit who will give the disciples the right word to say when they are called to defend themselves before heathen authorities. 'The Holy Spirit will teach you in that very hour what you ought to say' (Luke 12:12; also Matt. 10:20 and Mark 13:11 which stress that it will be the Spirit speaking through them). It is in the same context of gracious promise that the disciples are told to ask for the Spirit knowing that they will receive Him (Luke 11:13). The Spirit is to be theirs for the asking—without any preconditions apart from faith.

The promise reappears at the end of Luke's Gospel with the Lord directing the disciples to stay in Jerusalem until they receive the 'promise of the Father' (24:49). The future remains Christ's future, but His presence will now be given with the presence of the Spirit. He will be Christ's executor. It is significant that Matthew closes his gospel with the Great Commission which makes all disciples Christ's executors. The authority which belongs to Jesus by divine right and by the power of the Spirit is now vested in those He leaves behind. There is thus an implied promise of the Spirit. The disciples have the great mission of acting in the name and authority of Father, Son, and Holy Spirit (Matt. 28:19). The future age is the age of Father, Son, and Holy Spirit, not merely of the Spirit. The last promise remains: 'Lo, I am with you always, to the close of the age'.

However, the promise, the Gospel of the Spirit, is most clearly spelled out in **John's Gospel.** In the Farewell Discourses (John 14–16) shortly before His death, Jesus promises that the pain of present parting will be eased by the sending of the Paraclete, who will be the disciples' guide, advocate, and comforter in all they say and do. Whereas previously He had spoken of the Spirit of God, or the 'Spirit of your Father' (Matt. 10:20), it now becomes patently clear that the Spirit is also the Spirit of Jesus Himself. As we read through the five Paraclete-sayings, we note an interesting and deliberate progression. Jesus first speaks of the Father giving or sending the Paraclete, then of the Father sending Him 'in my name'. The climax comes with the promise: 'I shall send him to you' (John 14:16,26; 15:26; 16:7).

John also makes clear, even more clearly than do the other evangelists, that the Spirit will be the executor of Jesus Himself. Just as Christ is 'the truth' (14:6), so the coming Spirit is the 'Spirit of Truth' who will guide the disciples into all truth. 'For he will not speak on his own authority, but whatever he hears he will speak, and he will declare to you the things that are to come. He will glorify me, for he will take what is mine and declare it to you' (16:13–15). And so Jesus' words about the future worship of the Father also imply the promise of the Spirit. The new 'worship in spirit and in truth' (John 4:23,24) hardly means that future Christian worship will be new because worshippers will be genuine and sincere; both heathen and heretic are also usually sincere in their worship! No: the new access to the Father will rather be based on Christ who is the Truth and will be carried out in the power of the Spirit, not just a new human spirit.

It is John's Gospel which makes most clear the fact that Jesus' death and resurrection are, paradoxically, His glorification and enthronement in power. His death is not a sad end to the Spirit-filled Messiah, but rather the necessary presupposition to the full outpouring of the Spirit (John 7:39 and 16:7). And so it is only after the resurrection that Jesus breathes on His disciples, gives them His Spirit, and calls them into the new apostolate with its great commission to proclaim forgiveness (20:22,23). Now, at last, the call of Jesus in 7:37 ('If any one thirst, let him come to me and drink') can be answered. The glorification of Jesus means at the same time the sending of the Spirit (7:38,39). Thus the physical absence of the Messiah does not mean the loss of the Spirit in this world. It rather means a new presence in the person and work of His Spirit.

Chapter V

THE SPIRIT-FILLED CHURCH

1. The Acts of the Spirit

The book of Acts can be called the central pillar in the charismatic argument for a special baptism of the Spirit. Five passages figure very importantly in this argument. They are: the gift of the Spirit at Pentecost (chapter 2), to the Samaritans (chapter 8), to the Apostle Paul (chapter 9), to Cornelius and his household (chapters 10–11), and to the ex-disciples of John the Baptist at Ephesus (chapter 19). In three of these instances we also find an external sign of the Spirit's coming in the gift of tongues (Acts 2:4; 10:45; 19:6). About twelve years separates each of these last three events, so that, it is argued, there is no evidence that the special gift of the Spirit abated in the Early Church. Charismatics may differ among themselves about the necessity of tongues as a sign of the baptism of the Spirit, but all stress the special gift of tongues.

Though we shall concentrate on the above five key-passages, it will be helpful to begin with some remarks on the purpose of Luke in writing Acts, and with some notes on chapter 1 which provides the framework and prelude to the Pentecost story itself.

The charismatic movement has tended to make Acts the 'canon within the canon', and has often argued, or simply presupposed, that Luke's main concern is to answer the question: 'How does one become a Christian?', or 'How does one receive the Spirit?'. It is commonly presupposed that Acts gives us not only a picture of the ideal conditions in the Early Church, which should be emulated or repeated in the church today, but that Luke also outlines something like a set program on 'How to become a Christian'. His narrative, especially the various conversion stories, is thus viewed as providing precedents for a personalized *ordo salutis* (order of salvation) for all Christians, giving a chronological sequence of events from conversion to the Spirit-baptism, with tongues as a supernatural sign.

Now, no one will dare to deny that Luke has written *Heilsgeschichte* (salvation-history), to cite the German word used by scholars around the world. The preaching of the apostles continually demands the personal response of faith to the person of Jesus. Their message invokes personal questions of ultimate importance: 'Brethren, what shall we do?' (Acts 2:37), or, 'Men, what must I do to be saved?' (16:30). New Testament scholars have also pointed out that Luke has his own characteristic understanding of the nature of salvation. For him, the resurrection has become the event of salvation, so that he shows no real traces of Paul's theology of the cross. Nor does he (despite Acts 13:39) reflect the centrality of the doctrine of justification in the thought of St. Paul. Instead, he has his own stress on the saving power of 'the name' (see, for example, Acts 2:21,28,38; 3:6,16; 4:7,10–12,30).

However, Luke is interested in anything but a pattern of personal salvation. He writes the history of the church, its origins, its growth. We might even wish that he were a bit more systematic than he is in outlining the full significance and 'order' of the event of conversion, but that is not his purpose. He is concerned to show the growth of the church within the continuity of salvation-history, not to tell the story of individuals and their spiritual life. He is not even writing the Acts of the Apostles, as much as the Acts of the Lord through His Spirit.

We have seen Luke's special interest in the Spirit in his Gospel. While his Gospel presents us with the picture of the Spirit-filled Messiah, Acts pictures the Spirit-filled church. It is significant that Luke combines his resurrection and ascension Christology with his Pneumatology (his doctrine of the Spirit) right at the beginning of Acts in that programmatic statement in Peter's Pentecost sermon: 'This Jesus God raised up, and of that we are all witnesses. Being therefore exalted at the right hand of God, and having received from the Father the promise of the Holy Spirit, he has poured out this which you see and hear' (2:32,33). From the outset, it is vital to note that

> 'the discontinuity between Luke's gospel and his Acts is not marked by the creation of the church for the first time. It does not even consist in a new definition of church as such, but rather in a new confession to the Risen Lord, a new possession of his Spirit, and a new universal task, mission' (V. C. Pfitzner, 'The Lucan View of History in Acts', in *Theologia Crucis. Studies in Honour of Hermann Sasse*, Adelaide: Lutheran Publishing House, 1975, p. 38).

For Luke there is only one people of God in possession of the Spirit. Thus the justification of the Gentile mission is, in effect, the story of the Spirit and His guiding. From the story of Pentecost on, the church is clearly pictured not only as the Spirit-filled people of God, but also as Spirit-led. The apostles, as the original witnesses of the risen Lord, are filled with that particular gift of the Spirit: 'boldness' (*parrhesia*; 2:29; 4:13,29–31; etc.). The connection between the Spirit and the church as a whole comes to light in the story of Ananias and Sapphira. Their sin against the community of believers is a direct sin against the Spirit (Acts 5:3,9). The seven deacons are necessarily men 'full of the Spirit' (6:3).

It is even more important for our purpose to note that every stage in the church's expansion, according to the program enunciated in Acts 1:8, is initiated by the Spirit. The special Samaritan Pentecost in chapter 8 marks the inclusion into the church of these 'half-breeds' from the north. Philip's encounter with the Ethiopian eunuch is set up and terminated by the Spirit (8:29,39). Paul, the great missionary to the Gentiles, receives his special conversion-call with the filling of the Spirit (9:17). The same Spirit proves to the Jerusalem Jewish Christians that heathen people like Cornelius are also to be included in God's people without prior conditions apart from faith (10:44–11:18). It is naturally the Spirit who chooses Paul and Barnabas for the first missionary journey and sends them out (13:2–4), just as it is the Spirit who confirms their work (13:52). Finally, as we would expect, it is the

Spirit who is actually responsible for the Apostolic Decree at the Jerusalem Council (15:28), who continues to direct the missionaries at every turn in their future journeys (16:6,7).

'Led by the Spirit' might indeed be a good title for the whole book of Acts! For the moment, we simply note that Luke is interested in the growth of the church as the Spirit's work, not in the personal, spiritual growth of individuals as such. Conversions are narrated as part of an unfolding drama of salvation-history.

2. The Promise of the Spirit and Mission [Acts 1]

Luke consciously links his two writings by repeating Jesus' mission command (Luke 24:46–49 and Acts 1:8), the ascension (Luke 24:51 and Acts 1:9–11), and His promise of the Spirit (Luke 24:49 and Acts 1:4,5). He also connects both works in his introduction with the reference to Jesus having already spoken 'through the Holy Spirit' (Acts 1:1,2). The story about to be unfolded is still the story of Jesus who continues His work through His Spirit. 'The Spirit is Jesus at work in continuation of his ministry' (Bruner, *Theology of the Holy Spirit*, p. 156). We do not understand the role of the Spirit in Acts if we contrast His work with that of Christ, or see it as going beyond Christ and His work.

Acts 1 establishes the divine preconditions for the mission of the church about to begin. The repetition of the resurrection- and ascension-theme reminds us that the Christ who sent out His disciples is the living Lord who will come again. Christian mission is carried out in this perspective of the Gospel of Christ's return (1:11). But interwoven into the account of resurrection and glorification is the promise of the Spirit's coming (1:8). Finally (1:15–26) we have the re-establishment by the Lord Himself of the circle of the Twelve, the embryo of the people of God who were to be God's new servant in the world. It is important to see that all these preconditions for mission are met not by men, but by God. The command to wait in Jerusalem is an order to wait until God acts and provides the final precondition (1:4).

Charismatic literature makes much of the preconditions which must be met before the Spirit can be received. In particular, Acts 1:4 is used by Pentecostals to show the necessity of waiting on or 'tarrying' (from the AV) for the Holy Spirit. But this command does not demand any correct psychological or spiritual preconditioning on the part of man. There is no suggestion that only if they wait they will receive the Spirit. The emphasis is on Jerusalem. Luke sees Jerusalem as the central scene for the unfolding of the drama of redemption. This is the place of Christ's death and resurrection; this is the place where the Spirit must be poured out. The command of Jesus underscores the importance of Jerusalem in the divine plan, not the indispensability of the disciples' waiting!

Secondly, note that the Spirit is called 'promise' (*epangelia*). Beside Luke 24:49, Acts 1:4, 2:33 and 39, this word appears regularly as part of the Early Church's vocabulary of the Gospel, wherever grace is to be contrasted with human works or effort designed to merit something with God (see especially Rom. 4:13–26 and Gal. 3:13–29). From the beginning, the Spirit is spoken of as a free gift whose coming cannot be manipulated, induced, or 'turned on' by what man does.

Consequently, we find in Acts that other name for the Spirit: gift (*dorea*). He is God's good and perfect gift 'from above' (James 1:17), whose coming rests not with men but with God's gracious purpose. In passing, we recall how the related adverb (*dorean*) is used by Paul to stress that man, the sinner, is justified freely, by grace, through faith in Christ (Rom. 3:24). Acts, in all passages which show the outpouring of the Spirit, continually speaks of the Spirit as 'promise' or 'gift', as that which can never be earned or merited, but simply received (apart from 1:4, see also 2:33, 2:38,39; 8:20; 10:45; 11:17; 19:2).

We find here the same lack of conditions as in Luke 11:13—unless one wants to look upon asking and receiving as conditions! The promise is in the passive; 'until you are clothed with power' (Luke 24:49), or 'you shall be baptized' (Acts 1:5); the promise is absolute and unconditional. There is no limiting of the persons on whom the Spirit will fall, and no uncertainty when this will happen ('before many days'). The Spirit does not fall only on those who are properly prepared for Him at Pentecost, or at Ephesus (19:1–7).

It is important to note all this in order to see the simple objectivity of the promise of 1:8. The promise is the only precondition—not the prayer (1:14) or the 'tarrying' of the disciples, or any special soul-preparation or stage of sanctification.

3. The Miracle of Pentecost [Acts 2]

Was the Pentecost-outpouring a unique event, or was it the first example of what should happen in the life of every believer, namely a special experience of the Spirit after conversion? Pentecostals, and some neo-Pentecostals, stress that the disciples were already Christians before Pentecost; they were already 'clean' and their 'names . . . written in heaven' (Luke 10:20; John 13:10,11; 15:3; 20:22); thus the story of Pentecost is claimed to set a pattern for all Christians to follow. However, this interpretation does not do justice to the meaning of Pentecost within the framework of the whole book of Acts.

We have seen earlier how Luke pictures the Spirit as inaugurating stages in the plan of salvation-history, for example, with Jesus' birth and baptism. Acts 2 also pictures the inauguration of a new age in the history of the people of God. This is a special day, **the day** (2:1) which is **unique** in its **pivotal** importance (Dunn). It is indeed a watershed in salvation-history. When we see this point, we avoid the danger of understanding the miracle of Pentecost as an answer to the question: 'How can the individual receive the Spirit?'.

There is a close connection between Jesus' baptism and Pentecost. At the former, Jesus is designated the Spirit-filled Messiah, the new obedient Israel; at the latter, we have the fulfilment of the Joel prophecy and the establishment of the new Spirit-filled people of God. The Baptizer had expected the great baptism of the Spirit and fire with the coming of the Messiah. His questions from prison (Luke 7:18,19) seemed to indicate a growing doubt that Jesus was the fulfillment of this prophecy. Jesus answered with the assurance that the Spirit of the last times was indeed at work in Him, and referred to the Old Testament promise (Isa. 61:1; 35:5,6; 29:18,19). But, as yet, John's prophecy was not fully fulfilled.

Luke 12:49,50 shows in what way it was not yet fulfilled. The purificatory fire of judgment did not fall on Jesus at the Jordan—it could not fall on the Sinless One! And, yet, this passage indicates that Jesus longed for this fire also (note how the words 'fire' and 'baptism' occur together). The ministry of Jesus as the representative Servant of God was climaxed only by the baptism of fire in His passion. This was the cup of wrath that He must suffer for all men before the Spirit of renewal could be poured out.

This means that the New Covenant is fully established only with Pentecost. Up to this point there is (as there always has been, also in the Old Testament) the people of God; now there is church in the full New Testament sense. Between the ascension and Pentecost there was something like a 'pregnant pause'; there was no activity of the Spirit between these two events. Whereas Jesus had spoken to His disciples right up to the day of His ascension 'through the Holy Spirit' (Acts 1:2), there was now silence until 'the day' itself. The glorification of the Son was the only precondition for the full outpouring of the Spirit on the whole church (see again John 7:39).

The uniqueness of the Pentecost event is underlined by the use of the Joel prophecy by Peter, as recorded in Acts 2:17–21. Here, at last, is the great sign that the last days have begun.

James Dunn has pointed out the special covenantal significance of Pentecost in the following way (*Baptism in the Holy Spirit*, p. 47f.):

1. The Spirit is called the 'promise' (2:33,38,39; as in Luke 24:49 and Acts 1:4), the same word as used to designate the covenant promises given to God's people elsewhere (Acts 7:17; 13:23,32; 26:6; Rom. 4:13,16,20; 9:8; Gal. 3:14; etc.).

2. Luke, like Paul, seems to parallel the gift of the Spirit with the 'blessing of Abraham' (Gal. 3:14), since the wording of Acts 2:39 ('the promise is to you and to your children') is probably meant to recall the promise of the Abrahamic covenant (Gen. 17:7–10). This parallel becomes all the more likely as soon as we look at Acts 3:25. Through the gift of the Spirit at Pentecost, the nations of the earth who are to be blessed enter into a new covenant. 'All that are far off' (Acts 2:39) are already symbolized in the nations represented at this miraculous event.

3. The promise of the new covenant in Ezek. 36:27 and Jer. 31:33 included the promise of the Spirit. At Pentecost this promise becomes a reality.

4. There may be added significance in the fact that the Day of Pentecost in Judaism of the first century had come to be regarded not only as the Festival of First Fruits (harvest festival), but also as the commemoration of the giving of the Law on Mt. Sinai. This fact, if present in

Luke's mind, would also underline the thought that Pentecost was for the early Christians the beginning of a new covenant.

However, there is another way of showing that Pentecost is not a stage in the spiritual life of the disciples, but the beginning of a new era of the church. The church is there where there is confession to Christ as Lord (Acts 10:36; Rom. 10:9; 1 Cor. 12:3; Phil. 2:11 by implication). Acts shows that this confession was possible only after the Lord's ascension to glory (2:33). The confession of Peter at Caesarea Philippi was indeed a genuine Christological confession, but it arose not from Peter's faith or understanding, but had to be given to him. Even after the confession, Peter does not understand what he has actually said! The misunderstanding of the disciples until after Easter and Pentecost is, of course, a major feature of John's Gospel, but is found in the other Gospels as well. Again, the confession of believing Thomas in John 20:28 is a full Easter confession, but comes after Jesus has breathed His Spirit on the disciples. The church is not built up on man's confession, but on God's act. Thus it is only after Pentecost that the full Gospel call can be issued: 'Whoever calls on the name of the Lord shall be saved' (Acts 2:21; see how the key-words of this sentence are taken up in the rest of the chapter: 'call', 'name', 'Lord' and 'saved' recur in vv. 36,38–40, and 47).

In this connection it is significant that Luke follows the Pentecost story with the first of his so-called summary-reports (Acts 2:42–47; the others are 4:32–37 and 5:12–16). Here, and only here, do we find the essential marks of the church: the apostles' teaching; the fellowship (*koinonia*) that is the mark of the Spirit's presence in the church (2 Cor. 13:14; Phil. 2:1); and worship with the Sacraments of Baptism (v. 41) and the 'breaking of bread' (v. 42). The exact meaning of v. 42 is not quite clear, admittedly. The Greek word *koinonia* is also used for what we call the offering (see Rom. 15:26; 2 Cor. 8:4; 9:13); it can also be used for the communion or sharing which takes place at the Lord's Supper (1 Cor. 10:16). In any case, whether 'fellowship' here means the offering, the Eucharist, or even the sharing of things in common referred to in the following verses, and whether v. 42 refers to elements in the worship service of the early Christians or simply to marks of the church as such, we find here a description of the church as the people of God in possession of Christ's Spirit. Pentecost is thus not an initiatory experience for a chosen few who have met certain prior conditions of faith and piety; it is the beginning of a new fellowship as such. Thus, as we noted above, an offence against this fellowship is an offence against the Spirit Himself, a lying or tempting of the Spirit (5:3,9).

Finally, Peter's own words in Acts 10–11 underline our contention that Pentecost marks the beginning of the church with the beginning of faith in the full sense. Here we learn that Cornelius' experience of salvation was the same as that of the 120 at Pentecost. This means, to be quite precise, that the 120 were, before the reception of the Spirit, in the same state as was Cornelius, without that full faith which belongs to a Christian. Note the parallel stated in 11:15: 'The Holy Spirit fell on them just **as on us at the beginning**', and 11:17: 'God gave the same gift to them **as he gave to us when we believed** in the Lord Jesus Christ'. The last words of Peter in Acts 15:8–11 likewise show that, for Luke, the gift of the Spirit and coming to faith can never be separated. Luke uses the aorist tense in the above passages (and elsewhere) to describe the decisive coming to faith at an initial point of time see also 2:44; 9:42; 16:31). Whatever the relationship of the disciples was to the Lord in His earthly ministry, they were Christians in the full sense only after the gift of the Spirit at Pentecost. Pentecost is consequently the doorway of the church; it cannot be used to provide a pattern for Christian experience in terms of a sequence of events which must be followed. In a sense, this event is unrepeatable, and it certainly does not establish a law of precedent. What remains is the Gospel promise. For here, as always in Acts, the phrase 'to be baptized in/with the Spirit' means not a second experience over and above coming to faith, but the way to faith and the experience of conversion itself. It is always associated with entry into the Messianic age, just as Jesus' anointing with the Spirit at His baptism means His entry into His Messianic office.

The event of Pentecost is inclusive. 'They were **all** filled with the Holy Spirit' (2:4). No one was passed over because certain conditions had not been met. There could be no partial reception, since here also 'it is not by measure that he gives the spirit' (John 3:34); here also the gift that comes suddenly from above was good and perfect (James 1:17).

The event of Pentecost, like Jesus' baptism at the Jordan, is unique also in its individual features: the sound of a rushing wind, the tongues of fire (although Pentecostals claim to have sometimes seen these in our day). Only here do we hear of Christians speaking in 'other tongues', which, without argument, must be understood as intelligible languages (2:11). But the most important thing has yet to be said. The coming of the Spirit leads men to praise God's mighty deeds in His Son (2:11,22); here again, the function of the Spirit is to glorify Christ and the Father who sent Him.

To say it again, Luke sees the outpouring of the Spirit not as a personal experience of the original church-leaders, but as the fulfilment of promise of universal salvation. Acts 2 thus deals with the Gospel of salvation itself—nothing less; it certainly does not confront us with a second blessing after the reception of salvation.

A Note on Acts 2:37–39 and Baptism

What is the relationship between the gift of the Spirit and Baptism in Acts 2? Pentecostal interpretation grasps at 2:37–39 to argue for the doctrine of subsequence: first repentance, then faith expressed in Baptism, then the reception of the Spirit.

We briefly note the following. The Spirit produced both the sermon of Peter and the faith it called into being. That one cannot work out a neat sequence-theology at this point is clear from the fact that the hearers who had been convicted by the sermon were then told to repent. Obviously faith and repentance belong together as the work of the Spirit as always in Scripture (see Acts 13:48; 16:14; 18:27). And just as repentance and faith belong together, so do faith and Baptism. The hearers are actually not told to do something, but to **submit to** something ('be baptized', passive). That is the corollary of the Spirit's work. Baptism is not a work of man, but of the Spirit; it is received. Peter's words in full are:

> 'Repent, and be baptized every one of you in the name of Jesus Christ for the forgiveness of your sins; and you shall receive the gift of the Holy Spirit' (2:8).

That means, quite simply: 'Become a Christian by being baptized. And as a baptized Christian there is nothing surer than that you will receive the Spirit'. To avoid any confusion we should add: 'Be baptized and you will at the same time receive the Spirit!' The passage does not mention two baptisms, but one. Three thousand were baptized, and three thousand received the Spirit; the text is as simple as that. Any attempt to read into v. 38 a promise of the Spirit at some future time, after additional conditions have been met, destroys the Gospel promise of the text which is given in Baptism itself.

Further, Baptism is 'for the forgiveness of sins', not just a sign or symbol of forgiveness. And the scope of its effective promise is universal (v. 39); there is no temporal or national limitation to the gift of the Spirit. There is no mention of requirements on man's part—whether an emotional pitch, or stage of sanctification. The Spirit at work in Baptism clears the way for Himself.

Faith is the only condition for the Spirit's coming (Gal. 3:2). He is ours for the asking (Luke 11:13). Where this is not understood, Acts 5:32 is misunderstood. Here Peter says that the Holy Spirit is 'given to those who obey' God, a saying that is sometimes used to prove that obedience is a precondition for the reception of the Spirit. But the tenses show that obedience (present tense) follows the gift of the Spirit (past tense). There is a truth that the Spirit is poured out subsequent to obedience, but this is the 'obedience of faith' itself that Paul talks about in Rom. 1:5.

To summarize, we can do no better than listen to Bruner who writes:

> 'The exterior forms of Pentecost (wind, fire, visions, tongues) leave; the essential content remains. The content is God's free gift of the Holy Spirit. And after Pentecost this gift is offered . . . in the humble rite of baptism. Baptism becomes the baptism of the Holy Spirit. Peter . . . does not contrast baptism and the gift of the Spirit, he joins them.' (p. 168f.).

4. The Samaria Episode [Acts 8]

The strange events in Samaria have given rise to a whole series of different interpretations, reflecting the difficulties in understanding this passage. A certain ex-magician called Simon had created a stir in the city, and been called the 'power of God which is called Great' (8:10). If we remember that in the New Testament 'power' (*dynamis*) is a synonym for the Spirit, Simon's title assumes new importance. Whether he claimed to be the Spirit himself, or simply that he worked wonders through the Spirit, is not clear. What is clear is that Philip's preaching had an even greater effect on the Samaritans, who came to faith and were baptized. However, we soon find Peter and John in Samaria praying for the Samaritans 'that they might receive the Holy Spirit; for it had not yet fallen on any of them, but they had only been baptized in the name of the Lord Jesus' (8:15–16).

Here we seem to have a flat contradiction of what we have found in 2:38: that Baptism assures the reception of the Holy Spirit. Roman Catholic exegetes have sometimes overcome the problem by seeing here the practice of confirmation with the apostolic laying on of hands. Pentecostals have, on the other hand, found here a confirmation of their treasured doctrine of subsequence: first baptism, then the reception of the Spirit. At first sight this argument seems incontestable. It is literal, and obvious in its direct simplicity. Attempts to overcome the problem by arguing that, in fact, the Samaritans had received the Spirit and simply had to be assured of the fact by the Jerusalem apostles, or that they had received the Spirit but not the charismatic gifts, founder on the text and the clear statement of v. 16: the Spirit 'had not yet fallen on any of them'.

Luke's point is hardly to show that the giving of the Spirit was the sole prerogative of the apostles through the laying on of hands. According to 2:38, Baptism is the only rite necessary for the promise of the Spirit to be effected (see also 8:38; 10:48; 16:15,33; 18:8). In any case, that which characterized the apostles' ministry was not the administration of rites but eye-witness testimony (Acts 1:21,22). (Confirmation has, in fact, no direct biblical foundation, but is a ceremony instituted, whether for good or for bad, by the later church.) Again Acts shows that the laying on of hands is not an additional rite after Baptism but a part of it, a part of initiation into the faith as such (Acts 9:17–19; 19:5–6; Heb. 6:2). What the Samaritans lacked was not 'hands', but the Spirit! Finally, we note in passing that Ananias who lays his hands on Paul in 9:17 is not an apostle. The apostolic laying on of hands appears again only in 19:1–7. (However, even here we should remember that Paul, according to the Lucan definition of Acts 1:21,22, is not an apostle in the strict and original sense; he is called an apostle only twice in Acts (14:4,14), and then in connection with Barnabas who also was not an original Jerusalem eye-witness.) Again, in the Acts 19 passage, what was lacking was not 'hands', but Baptism. The laying on of hands was probably simply a symbol of prayer for the Spirit (8:15 and 8:17 belong together).

In his *Baptism in the Holy Spirit* (pp. 63–68), James Dunn rightly argues that Luke wants to show in this event the decisive difference between pseudo-faith and genuine faith, not a correct sequence of events in Christian experience. As in all the Spirit-passages in Acts, he is illustrating the way in which a person becomes a Christian; he is talking about the original entry into the Kingdom. Dunn further suggests that here we have an extraordinary situation which only serves to prove Luke's point that the reception of the Spirit is synonymous with becoming a Christian.

Dunn's argument, in brief, is as follows: Philip's preaching and baptizing were hardly defective. What was defective was the faith of the Samaritans

The Samaritans also had their own form of Messianic hope. Both the activity of Simon and of Philip touched off a sudden movement of excited expectation that the *Taheb* (as they called the Messiah) was coming. But Philip's preaching outdoes that of Simon. They hear the 'good news . . . about the name of Jesus Christ' (a strange phrase!) and associate this Messiah with their previous hope. Luke, says Dunn, deliberately draws the appearance of Simon and Philip together, describing the reaction of the people to both men in similar terms (vv. 6 and 10,11).

Secondly, their reaction is described with a strange phrase, 'they believed Philip' (*episteusan tō Philippō*), a use of the verb which normally describes belief in a proposition or statement, not the commitment of faith in Christ (v. 12). It is a word-usage unique in Luke's Greek.

The conclusion is clear. Before the apostles came up from Jerusalem, the Samaritans were not even Christians. Thus Luke does not involve himself in any kind of contradiction. The case of Simon who 'believes' and 'is baptized', but is unmasked as an unbeliever, seems to prove the truth of the argument. What is clear is that Simon finally has no part in salvation (v. 21), a fact that is asserted in Old Testament terms (Ps. 78:37 and Isa. 58:6 stand behind vv. 21–23). The problem was not that he was partly a Christian (faith and baptism without the Spirit), but that he was from the outset only a Christian in name. That is the tragedy of this man who came to be regarded by early Christians as the arch-heretic. That he thinks he can buy the Spirit shows how little he understands the Gospel. The Spirit remains pure gift. Simon certainly illustrates the sad truth that merely claiming the name of Christ does not validate the claim to the Spirit. Nor does Baptism without true faith.

But the question remains: Was the faith of the Samaritans really deficient, as Dunn maintains? This is hardly likely in view of the clear statement of v. 12. Their baptism was evidently valid, for they were not re-baptized by the apostles. The solution to the problem is to take the text quite literally. Two conclusions will follow from a careful analysis of the Samaria episode within the framework of the story of Acts and Luke's theological argument.

1. We surely have here another unique episode in the story of Acts, the growth of the church from Jerusalem to Rome under the direction of the Spirit. The region of Samaria had been singled out in Acts 1:8 for special mention in the program for the church's mission. Here then is a pivotal point in salvation-history. Indeed, we should go further. This event is not simply unique; it is nothing less than extraordinary! We are compelled to take this position since Luke (like Paul in Gal. 3:2) believes that becoming a Christian and receiving the Spirit are one and the same thing. And yet, here we seem to have Christians who do not have the Spirit! How do we explain this?

It is an obvious fact that Luke shows a special interest in the Samaritans, also in his Gospel. He alone has the story of the Good Samaritan (Luke 10:30–37), and the story of the thankful Samaritan leper who came back to Jesus (17:11–19). Only Luke tells us about Jesus' refusal to call down divine punishment on a Samaritan village which refused to accept Jesus' disciples (Luke 9:51–56). Clearly Acts 9:31 indicates, as much as does 1:8, that Samaria is a decisive stage in the history of the church.

Now, when we recall what the Samaritan meant for the Jew, we can easily understand how a special event was necessary to convince the Jerusalem Jewish Christians that the Samaritans were indeed to be accepted as full members of the church. As in the Cornelius story, where the Jerusalem Christians are the ones who had to learn a lesson (10:45) from the Gentiles' reception of the Spirit, so here we have nothing less than an extraordinary event designed to leave an indelible impression on the first Christians: the old religious barriers between Judaism and Samaritanism are done away with!

Verse 16, consequently, does not set a normal pattern, but establishes an extraordinary situation. The words **not yet** and **only** are emphatic and indicate the temporary suspension of the normal, namely, that faith, Baptism, and the reception of the Spirit belong together, not in terms of a rigid sequence (the freedom of the Spirit would speak against such an idea) but of one gracious action of God through His Spirit. Thus, Baptism and receiving the Spirit are not contrasted by Luke, but correlated.

2. Luke is also concerned in Acts with the unity and continuity of the church. Jerusalem was the mother-church and the home of the apostles, the witnesses of the risen Lord. And the church's growth remained anchored to eye-witness testimony. That was why the apostles Peter and John figured in this episode, just as they did in that other new stage in the church's mission, the inclusion of the Gentiles. We should carefully note how 8:14 offers an exact linguistic parallel to 11:1. In both cases the apostles heard of the reception of the Gospel in a new territory; in both bases they were soon on the scene to confirm the fact that this had indeed happened. The apostles were not the guarantors of the Spirit, but the original witnesses to Christ. The delayed gift of the Spirit shows to them as well as to the Samaritans and to Philip himself, that this new stage in mission is Spirit-directed! No church arose that was not knit together with the earliest group of Christians who had received the Spirit. It is a mark of the church, as Ephesians reminds us (2:11–22), that the old national barriers have been overcome in Christ who is the headstone. But the apostles remain the foundation stones (Eph. 2:20).

Acts 8:18–24, as powerfully as any passage in Acts, illustrates the truth that the Spirit is always a gift. Simon's error is that he does not understand the Gospel of grace. Any charismatic interpretation of Acts which talks much of 'power', even if power for service, and does not see that the gift of the Spirit is the gift of salvation itself, misreads Acts. And Rom. 11:35,36 is as relevant here as in any situation where men want to place conditions on the reception of God's good and perfect gifts. 'Who has ever made a gift to him, to receive a gift in return?' The answer must be an unconditional 'no one'!

A Note on the Ethiopian Eunuch [Acts 8:26–40]

The story of the Samaritans does not record any charismatic manifestations with the Spirit's coming; nor does the following account of the conversion of the eunuch climax in a speaking-in-tongues or the like. Of course, silence is no proof that this did not take place; but, if Luke had wanted to show (as has been argued) that speaking in tongues is the normal evidence of the Spirit's coming, it is hard to understand why Luke should have omitted any reference to it.

Clearly the Spirit is at work in this new incident, which is something like an overture to the full Gentile mission to come later. The Spirit is mentioned twice in the course of the narrative, but both times in connection with Philip, not with the eunuch (v. 29,39). At the same time, Luke hints at the Spirit's power in the conversion of the man himself. The eunuch was convinced of the truth of the Gospel of Jesus Christ from his reading of Scripture (Isa. 53). Obviously Philip's teaching included instruction on the way into the Kingdom. Verse 37 presupposes this. The Spirit has arranged and terminated the meeting, but after the man is baptized, the evidence of the Spirit's work remains—not in tongues, but in joy. The eunuch becomes a Christian, and goes on his way rejoicing (v. 39). Joy is not only an important theme in Luke's two works, it is also the fruit of the Spirit (Acts 11:23,24; 13:52; Gal. 5:22).

The gift of the Spirit is not expressly mentioned (although later Greek manuscripts inserted a mention of this in v. 39 as well as a confession to Jesus as the Son of God and the Christ in v. 37). Nor are faith and repentance mentioned. That these three things are missing need not surprise us at all, since to speak of Baptism is to include all three other points. We see again that there is only one experience of conversion by which a heathen man comes into the Kingdom—by Word and Sacrament. There is no separation of Baptism and the Spirit.

5. The Conversion of Paul [Acts 9]

Again, the Pentecostal argument which uses Acts 9 appears to be sound at first sight. Paul is converted on the road to Damascus, and only three days later receives the Spirit. Here, surely, is a clear case of subsequence. In addition, we have further proof, so we are told, that this is the normal pattern, since God would not have given this experience to the great apostle to the Gentiles, were it not also promised to all Christians. Here is the equipping of Paul with power for ministry (a typical charismatic phrase).

At least we can agree, in part, to the last thought—with a proviso. It is made quite clear that Paul is not equipped with supernatural manifestations to convince his hearers of the truth of his message. What is stated is that he is being called and will be equipped for a ministry of suffering. 'I will show him how much he must suffer for the sake of my name' (9:16). Later, near the end of his ministry, Paul himself says to the elders of Ephesus as he bids them farewell:

> 'And now, behold, I am going to Jerusalem, bound in the Spirit, not knowing what shall befall me there; except that the Holy Spirit testifies to me in every city that imprisonment and afflictions await me' (20:22,23).

Remember again how just this was one of the bones of contention between Paul and the Corinthians; they challenged his apostolic authority since to them he did not appear to be able to authenticate his ministry with the right external power. He answers, as we noted above (chapter II, section 3), by referring to divine strength made perfect in human weakness, by pursuing a theology of the Cross, not a theology of glory which demands signs and demonstrations of power.

But the basic question remains: Do we have once more, in Acts 9, the doctrine of subsequence? Put quite simply, did Paul first become a Christian, and then receive the Spirit and power for witness? In answering the charismatic position, it will not be sufficient merely to point out that the usual sequence seems to be reversed; the text at first seems to suggest that Paul first received the Spirit and only then was baptized (vv. 17,18). Even if this were the case as in 10:44–48, the Pentecostal will readily admit that even today, as in New Testament times, the Spirit is free to change the order as long as man still experiences the 'full spirit'.

Those who say that Paul was a full Christian on the Damascus road argue that Paul addressed Jesus with the Christological confession 'Lord' (v. 5), and that Ananias greeted him as 'brother', as a fellow-Christian (v. 17; for this use see 22:13). *Kyrios* (Lord) was a title of respect commonly used in New Testament times without any Christological connotations. But, quite apart from this, Paul can hardly be making a Christian confession when he does not know to whom he is talking. Secondly, the term 'brother' is also the usual title for a fellow-Jew. Nineteen times it is used in Acts for Jewish kinship, and only becomes a standard word for 'fellow-Christian' after 9:30, as has been pointed out.

More important than these details is the fact that Luke hardly pictures the importance of a sequence of events. The whole story (9:1–18) tells us simply of Paul's conversion as one event. Paul's blindness, which is surely also symbolical of his prior state, is removed only after three days (vv. 9 and 18). Certainly Ananias speaks about the Spirit whom Paul will receive as he lays his hands on Paul (we are using his later name throughout), but the action is first related to the promise that he will regain his sight. Verse 17 does not say that Paul immediately received the Spirit and only then was baptized. Acts 22:13 and 16 show the same sequence: the regaining of sight and finally baptism. That the reception of the Spirit is not mentioned in this second account of Paul's conversion only suggests that for Luke Paul's baptism was indeed the point where he became a full Christian, with the reception of the Holy Spirit.

Against all this, it might be argued that Paul was still commissioned on the Damascus road. And how can one be called to be a missionary without first being a Christian? But a close look at the three accounts of Paul's conversion in Acts 9, 22, and 26, shows that Luke (and Paul) made no neat distinction on the exact moment of his commissioning. In chapter 9 it is actually Ananias who commissions Paul; in 22:14,15 this is again the situation, though it is presupposed that Christ had already called him directly in his Damascus experience. In chapter 26 Ananias is not mentioned at all; we simply read that Christ 'appointed' Paul for his great mission (26:16). In short, Paul's whole experience, including his conversion, call, and commissioning, from the vision on the road to his baptism, is a unity. The whole three days constitute one experience, in which the various stages or sequences of events have no specific significance or importance; Paul has had one great experience—he has become a Christian! And the *unique* thing about this conversion is that it was accompanied by a call to a universal mission.

There is no point in attempting to psychologize Paul's conversion or his blindness. The latter surely has a deeper significance than being mere physical ailment (cf. John 9:39–41, Acts 26:18; 2 Cor. 4:4–6), and cannot be simply explained as a reaction from shock or the like. Paul himself never gives a psychological explanation of his conversion. Phil. 3:4–7 recalls Paul's past not as a period in which he was spiritually desperate before his conversion, but one in which he was proud to be a Jew and confident that he was keeping the Law. There was no preparation, humanly speaking, for Paul's conversion and reception of the Spirit. Paul was stopped dead in his tracks, as we say. He was pressed into God's service without meeting any preconditions of faith, piety, and holiness. No wonder that he understood so well the gift of faith, of Baptism, of the Spirit, of the total Gospel as grace and nothing but pure grace!

6. The Conversion of Cornelius [Acts 10–11]

Here again, in Acts 10–11, according to the charismatic argument, Cornelius first became a Christian by hearing the Word, and then received the Spirit, as did others of his household. The key-question is again: Is the experience of conversion separate from the gift of the Spirit? The other important question is: What is the place of this story in the program of Acts?

We must again insist that this event is recorded by Luke because of its pivotal importance for salvation-history. The Gentile mission had been foreshadowed earlier in Acts and was contained in the mission command and promise of Jesus in 1:8. The conversion of the Ethiopian eunuch was something like an overture to the Gentile mission. But this episode is crucial for the history of the Early Church, for it not only establishes, by the proof of the Spirit, that the Gentile mission is the will of the Lord; it also answers the basic question which Paul had to answer in his letters: Are the Gentiles on the same level as the circumcised (Jews) when it comes to the reception of grace, to the reception of the Spirit? That this question is answered by the Cornelius story is clear from Peter's vision (10:9–16) and the subsequent development of the theme of the 'cleanness' and acceptability of the Gentiles (v. 28,34). But Peter's vision was only the first stage of the lesson which the Jerusalem church leaders had to learn.

It is interesting to note that, just as Philip was led by the Spirit to the eunuch, so here it is the Spirit who arranges the meeting with Cornelius (10:19,20; 11:12–14). Luke was not laying down precedents for normal Christian experience, but was recording a very special occurrence of unique significance in the history of the Early Church as the Spirit led the church into all truth, including an understanding of the dimensions of its mission. Thus the special sign of the Spirit (tongues, v. 46) was meant to prove a point not for Cornelius and his household, but for the Jewish Christians. It is they who were amazed that the Spirit had been poured out '**even** on the Gentiles' (v. 45). It was the Jerusalem believers who had to be told in 11:17 that the Gentiles' experience of the Spirit was no different from that experienced by the circumcision-party. 'God gave the **same gift** to them as he gave to us **when we believed** in the Lord Jesus Christ.'

The absolute grace-character of the Spirit is clear from the text. While Peter was still preaching the Gospel (without any mention of a promised Spirit), the Spirit fell on Cornelius and his household. The Spirit simply came with faith. It is furthermore clear from 11:14–17 that the very gift of salvation was not something separate from the gift of the Spirit, but identical with it. All that Peter said in the summary report in 11:14–18 is: Cornelius and others had become Christians; the Spirit had shown that quite clearly.

It is significant that the very last words of Peter in Acts are these: 'We believe that we shall be saved through the grace of the Lord Jesus, just as they [that is, the Gentiles] will' (15:11). This event was for Peter and the other apostles the decisive proof that the only condition for becoming a Christian was the reception of the Spirit. Thus the Gentile mission was not an optional extra for the Early Church.

While we have a special outpouring of the Spirit on Gentiles, it still does not prove that Baptism and the reception of the Spirit are always two separate events. The order of the Spirit's coming belongs to His divine freedom, but it is vital to note that Cornelius and the others with him are still baptized **after** they have spoken in tongues. The Spirit can come prior to Baptism (here), after Baptism (19:5–6), or with Baptism (2:38), but **never apart from** Baptism and the Word. Peter shows that he could not associate the gift of the Spirit with the preaching of the Word alone (v. 48). The sign of the Spirit's presence in tongues did not lead him to reject Baptism; that was the one sure place where the Spirit would be given.

7. Apollos and the Disciples at Ephesus [Acts 18–19]

Acts 18:24–19:7 is the last key-passage in Acts which belongs to the charismatic arsenal of proof-passages used to prove the doctrine of subsequence. Apollos knows only John's baptism, yet is still 'fervent in Spirit' (18:25). He does, of course, need further instruction to know 'the way of God more accurately' (v. 26). But according to charismatics, what he and the Ephesians (who also knew only John's baptism, 19:3) really needed was not Christian Baptism, but the Spirit. It is argued that the Ephesians were fully Christian; after all, they are called disciples and believers (19:1,2). Verse 2 is taken to mean that it was the normal thing that they did not receive the Spirit when they were baptized. They, like Apollos (even though this is not expressly stated with reference to him), have to go through the right stages before they can receive the Spirit **after** their conversion. The **conditions** have to be met. Finally, it is argued, the Spirit is again given only with the laying on of hands by Paul after the Ephesians have been baptized.

The key-question is again: Were the Ephesians really Christians before they were baptized and received the Spirit? The answer must be a definite No! The story of Apollos and of the Ephesians must be read together, for in chapter 19 we are still in 'Apollos territory' (see 18:24); the problem was the same in both cases. They knew only the baptism of John. They certainly knew about Christ, but it is going too far to call them Christians. In 19:1 Luke calls them 'some disciples' without using the definite article which is used to denote Christians as disciples. The fact that Paul **called** them believers was, in fact, no proof that they **were**. They soon proved to be not so, and were thus baptized in the name of Jesus. What they lacked was not just the Spirit, but Christian faith, conversion, Baptism, and Spirit! (Some commentators have suggested that these people were still, in fact, disciples of John the Baptist. We know that a Baptizer sect lived on well after these times, but it cannot be proved beyond doubt that this solution is correct. All we are told is that these people knew only John's baptism.)

The crucial verse is v. 2. 'Did you receive the Holy Spirit when you believed?' Paul here applies the same test of Christianity as he does in Gal. 3:2. If these two passages are not to stand in complete contradiction, we have to say that Paul was nothing less than amazed that these people whom he presumed were Christians had not received the Spirit. His further questioning revealed the problem. The coming of the Spirit was linked not to John's baptism, but to Baptism 'in the name of the Lord Jesus' (v. 5).

Paul did not say that they had heard a false Gospel or a half-Gospel. He did not go on to say that what they lacked was the apostolic laying on of hands. He did not say something like, 'You are still not holy enough, you still do not believe enough'. The remedy for the lack of the Spirit was as simple as it was instantaneous. Paul immediately baptized the Ephesians. The gift followed Baptism without a time-lag. They became Christians, and they received the Spirit; the two, as always, go hand in hand. Here is the clearest proof that Luke understands Baptism in Jesus' name as the fulfilment of the Pentecost promise.

The laying on of hands here cannot be used to prove two comings or experiences of the Spirit. What the exact significance of this action was, is difficult to say. But we can understand why it should have occurred at Samaria and Ephesus. The physical action is best understood as a symbol of transferral of divine power in an act of prayer, just as anointing with oil in the Old Testament symbolized the gift of the Spirit. Whatever its exact significance, there is no suggestion that the Spirit was given only through this rite. The Spirit remains God's magnificent gift to man in the event of conversion/Baptism itself.

The Summary of Acts

To sum up briefly our findings in the book of Acts, we affirm the following:

1. Acts does not set out steps for Christian growth and experience, but tells the story of the growth of the church in the ever-widening circle of the experience of salvation itself.
2. The promise of John and Jesus about the coming Spirit is fulfilled unconditionally at Pentecost, and every time others come to faith.
3. There is no such thing as a 'baptism of/in the Spirit' as a second experience of grace. The reception of the Spirit is the same as the reception of salvation.
4. The gift of the Spirit is pure grace. There are no conditions to be met by man for His reception—apart from coming to faith in the first place. And this is also the work of the Spirit.
5. The one place where the Christian can be sure he has received the Spirit is in his baptism in the name of Jesus. The so-called 'baptism in the Spirit' is not a subsequent experience of grace, but grace itself.
6. Apparent irregularities in Acts (at Samaria and Pentecost) only confirm the above findings, and point, moreover, to the special character of certain events which are break-through points in the mission of the church.

Chapter VI

FAITH AND LIFE—THE SPIRIT'S WORK

Paul and the other writers of the New Testament Letters have little of Luke's interest in documenting the growth of the church as a historical process. Their concern is to proclaim and teach the Gospel, and what it means for the readers in their own special circumstances. They are theologians; but they are, above all, pastors seeking to deepen faith, warn against error, encourage in suffering, and inspire to holiness of living. They write to believers, as those who already have the Spirit of God, who have already experienced His grace. One thing can be said with certainty from the outset: **there is not one command in the New Testament Letters** (or the book of Revelation) **to seek a filling with the Spirit, or a special second experience.**

One thing must surely strike us as we read Paul's letters. How often must he not have shaken his head and even wrung his hands over the errors of his converts? But even where there was error and downright heresy, he always presupposed that his readers were Christians, that they possessed faith, that they had the Spirit—yes, even where the truth had been distorted, and the Spirit's gifts had been abused!

It is especially in the so-called Four Chief Letters of Paul (Romans, 1 and 2 Corinthians and Galatians) that he develops the doctrine of the Holy Spirit and His gracious work. And, as we have already noted, he does this in the process of fighting against distortions of the Gospel. In all four Letters, the doctrine of the Spirit is integrally connected with his struggle for the doctrine of justification by grace, through faith in Christ. In the case of Romans and Galatians, we find a thorough statement of the Gospel of grace against the Judaizing error which insisted on the 'extra' of obedience to the Law in addition to the obedience of faith for justification. In the Corinthian Letters, we find Paul fighting against an error which smacks more of Hellenistic influences, against a 'spiritualism' which threatened the Gospel in another way.

Two points are here significant: 1. In both cases, Paul argues not only with the Gospel itself, but also with instruction on the Spirit; the Spirit is part of the Gospel. 2. He has to argue thus because, in both errors, we have the idea of something added to the Gospel.

1. The Spirit and the Gospel of Baptism

It is, perhaps, best to begin with that passage of Paul which is used by charismatics to argue that he also taught a second baptism, one with the Spirit. In 1 Cor. 12:12,13 Paul writes:

> 'Just as the body, is one and has many members, and all the members of the body, though many, are one body, so it is with Christ. For by one Spirit we were all baptized into one body—Jews or Greeks, slaves or free—and all were made to drink of one Spirit.'

This is the only instance of the phrase 'to be baptized in/with the Spirit' outside of the Gospels and Acts. We need not argue whether the Greek preposition *en* means 'in' or 'with'; it can mean both. The issue is whether we have here one or two baptisms. We observe the following:

a) The body referred to here is the Body of Christ, the church.

b) Paul is arguing the unity of the church, and the Spirit as the source of special gifts. Despite the diversity of gifts and the plurality of members in the body, the body is one, just as the Spirit is one (see the phrase 'same Spirit' in 12:4,8,9; 'one Spirit' in v. 9; 'one and the same Spirit' in v. 11).

c) Entry into this Body, the church, is via Baptism 'by/in one Spirit'. This Baptism is quite clearly baptism with water in which the Spirit is at work.

d) 'We were all baptized' indicates that Baptism is not the experience of a select few, but the experience of all Christians, all members of the body.

e) This is underlined by a typical Pauline reference to the totality and unity of the church as 'Jews or Greeks, slaves or free' (Gal. 3:28; Col. 3:11; see also Eph. 2:13–18).

f) The final phrase must be seen as explaining the significance of Baptism itself, not a second experience of the Spirit. It parallels the statement at the beginning of the verse (v. 13). We must say this because the little word 'all' refers to the same people who have been baptized, not a second group who have 'all' had another experience.

g) The verb 'drink' again uses the biblical image of the Spirit as water (John 7:37–39). We are again reminded of the fact that in the Bible the experience of salvation is often pictured in terms of eating and drinking (see, for example, 1 Peter 2:2,3, but especially Heb. 6:4).

To sum up: There is here only one baptism in the Spirit, and that is the water-Spirit Baptism by which every Christian has been implanted or incorporated into the body of Christ (Rom. 6:3,4; Col. 2:12; Gal. 3:27). The gifts of the Spirit arise, consequently, not from a baptism of the Spirit as distinct from Baptism with water, but from the experience of grace itself. *Charismata* are special, individual gifts of the Spirit which presuppose the basic and most important gift of all, *charis* (grace).

We come, then, to the same conclusion that we reached in looking at the Gospels and Acts. But what of Hebrews 6:2? Charismatics (especially Pentecostals) argue that this verse speaks of two distinct baptisms since the Greek text speaks of 'instruction about *baptismoi*', the latter being plural in number.

Here knowledge of New Testament Greek is important. The RSV rightly translates the Greek word *baptismoi* with 'ablutions' or 'washings'—not 'baptisms', for which the New Testament word is *baptismata*. *Baptismoi* is found also in Mark 7:4 and Heb. 9:10 where it clearly refers to ritual washings for purification, the kind of washings that are referred to with the verb 'to baptize' in the Greek Old Testament (the Septuagint) at Judith 12:7 and Sirach 34:30. Mark 7:4 speaks of the 'washing of cups and pots and vessels of bronze', while Heb. 9:10 refers to washings of the body which are a part of the Jewish Old Testament cult. It would be most unusual for the word to mean one thing in this verse and another in Heb. 6:2. The unknown writer of the Letter to the Hebrews knew that his readers had known many washings and purificatory rites. They doubtless knew also of John's baptism in the past, as well as Christian Baptism. But all these are not *baptismata*, but *baptismoi*; there is finally only one Baptism (Eph. 4:5)!

It is argued that the writer cannot mean Jewish ritual-washings since Heb. 6:1 speaks about 'doctrines of Christ'; the washings or 'baptisms' must therefore be Christian, not Jewish. But this argument is easily countered with two observations.

First, the Letter to the Hebrews was written to Jewish Christians (that they were called Hebrews perhaps indicates that they were still Aramaic-speaking), who had to be taught the absolute superiority of Christ over Moses and the Old Testament cult with its sacrificial system; references to Jewish ritual-washings would be in no way out of place.

Secondly, all the teachings listed in 6:1,2 were not distinctive Christian teachings; they had their Jewish counterpart. The writer was thus saying: It should not be necessary for me to run through the range of Christian teachings all over again to explain what they mean in contrast to Jewish teaching.

Neither language nor logic allows us to insert here a teaching of a second baptism of the Spirit. The New Testament truth remains clear and unassailable: There is only one baptism of the Spirit, the experience of salvation itself in Baptism.

It has been argued that our interpretation of 1 Cor. 12:13 still does not rule out a second filling of the Spirit, for, while the text speaks of a baptism by the Spirit, it does not speak of a filling or receiving of the Spirit. We find a distinction in charismatic thinking between the experience of the Spirit's power in conversion (for salvation), and the infilling of the Spirit with power (for service and witness). Is this a biblical distinction?

In showing the Corinthians how to live a life of God-pleasing holiness, Paul does not wield the big stick of the Law. He reminds them of the Gospel-fact that they have become different and thus should live different lives. The old maxim applies: Be what you are! To those who have abused their bodies in sexual licence, he writes:

> 'Do you not know that your body is a temple of the Holy Spirit within you, which you have from God? You are not your own; you were bought with a price. So glorify God in your body.' (1 Cor. 6:19,20; see also 7:23).

The phrase 'bought with a price' is a clear reference to Christ's vicarious death. At a definite point of time, Christ had died for sinners; at a definite point of time in the readers' past, this death (and the consequent life) had become theirs. Since their conversion their bodies were temples of the Spirit and under the lordship of Christ. Paul is saying: 'As Christians who have been saved and have the Holy Spirit, you are under new management, new ownership. Acknowledge that fact with your life'.

That 1 Cor. 6:19,20 refers to one experience of salvation is proved by looking a few verses earlier in the same chapter. Paul recalled the kind of life his readers had lived while they were still heathen, citing sins that were typical of their pagan past. He then continued: 'Such were some of you. But you were washed, you were sanctified, you were justified in the name of the Lord Jesus Christ and in the Spirit of our God' (6:11).

All three verbs in this climactic sentence are in the past passive tense. They point to a single complete action of God, to that moment when the Corinthian readers became Christians. 'Washed', 'sanctified', 'justified', all point to one event with its various meanings. They have been cleansed from sin, set apart as holy, and declared just (forgiven). The verb used for 'washing' occurs only one other time in the whole of the New Testament, in Acts 22:16 where Ananias says to Paul, 'Rise and be baptized, and wash away your sins, calling on his [Christ's] name'. The related noun appears in Titus 3:5 where the doublet 'washing of regeneration and renewal in the Holy Spirit' clearly refers to Baptism. If we put all three texts together (1 Cor. 6:11; Acts 22:16; Titus 3:5) we find three common elements in Baptism: the name of Jesus, washing away of sins, and the Spirit.

The conclusion is clear: the single past event in 1 Cor. 6:11 is not a different or prior event to that referred to in 6:19,20; the believer has the Spirit within him by virtue of his baptism in the name of Jesus. He has not merely experienced the eternal power of the Spirit; the Spirit is his in all His fullness. Whether that Spirit is allowed to rule in the believer as He wants to is another matter. But the Gospel of the possession of the Spirit in Baptism is something that must be stressed and cherished in order to avoid the error of imagining that the Spirit is given in His fullness only in a second experience.

2. The Assurance of Faith

How does one receive the Spirit? Our first answer has been: in Baptism. If we now give a second answer: by faith, this should not be seen as involving us in a contradiction. For the benefits of Holy Baptism are themselves received by faith.

We have at various points referred to Gal. 3:2 as something like Paul's central statement on the reception of the Spirit. Galatians, Paul's charter of Christian liberty, shows the apostle in a no-holds-barred attack on an error which tries to add something extra to faith as the one precondition for salvation by God's justifying act in His Son. In other words, all that is needed for the sinner to receive God's verdict which declares him just, is to accept that verdict in faith. The Judaizers had tried (and apparently with some success) to convince the Galatians that they must also obey the Law—in particular, that they must retain the practice of circumcision. Paul's fundamental answer was given in Gal. 2:16: '[We] know that a man is not justified by works of the law but through faith in Jesus Christ, even we [who] have believed in Christ Jesus, . . . because by works of the law shall no one be justified'. Not only can no man keep the Law perfectly, it is not God's will that he try to justify himself in this way. For He has prepared another way: the Gospel proclaims the gift of righteousness in Christ as pure unmerited grace. Nothing can be added to faith in Christ for the reception of God's declaration of the sinner as a saint.

In 1 Cor. 1:18–2:5 Paul illustrated the truth of a thesis (1:18) by referring to the readers themselves, their situation, and their call to faith. Here in Galatians Paul has done the same thing. He goes on from his central statement in 2:16 to illustrate its truth from the example of the Galatians themselves (3:1,2):

> 'O foolish Galatians! Who has bewitched you, before whose eyes Jesus Christ was publicly portrayed as crucified? Let me ask you only this: Did you receive the Spirit by works of the law [that is, by obedience to the Law], or by hearing with faith [that is, from the Gospel which you heard and received in faith]?'

There is hardly any clearer statement in the whole of the New Testament of the equation: **to become a Christian = to receive the Spirit**. The second equation must therefore be: **to be a Christian = to have the Spirit.** This truth is further underlined in Paul's following words:

> 'Having begun with the Spirit, are you now ending with the flesh? Did you experience so many things in vain? . . . Does he who supplies the Spirit to you and works miracles among you do so by works of the law, or by hearing with faith?' (3:3–5).

God supplies His Spirit freely out of grace. It is important to note that faith itself, and not signs or miracles, is the 'proof of the Spirit', for it is God who both supplies the Spirit and works miracles. It could, of course, be objected that God works miracles **through** the Spirit. But the evidence of the Spirit's presence among the Galatians is not seen in the miracles as such, but in the very fact that the Galatians are believers. Thus, in the same letter Paul can equate the phrase 'through the Spirit' with 'by faith' (Gal. 5:5).

There are at least four other observations which show that the Spirit is received by faith without any extras, whether obedience, piety, prayer, or the like.

1. The work of Christ and that of the Spirit are inseparably connected in Paul's writings. Paul can say at one moment that the Spirit intercedes for us, and in the next moment speak of Christ as intercessor (Rom. 8:16 and 34). This is no contradiction, but rather enforces the truth that the Spirit and His work in the church is the assurance of the personal presence of Christ Himself. Paul can also speak of the indwelling of Christ and the indwelling of the Spirit in the same breath (Rom. 8:9–11 and Eph. 3:16–19). To be aglow with the Spirit means to serve Christ the Lord (Rom. 12:11).

There is here no cult of the Spirit, or of certain gifts which can be seen apart from the experience of salvation itself. Rather, the Father witnesses to the Son, the Son to the Father, and it is the crown of the Spirit's work that He produces the great confession of faith to the Son. For 'no one can say "Jesus is Lord" except by the Holy Spirit' (1 Cor. 12:3).

Paul is not alone in equating the indwelling of Christ and His Spirit. The apostle John says precisely the same thing (1 John 3:24 and 4:13). Like Paul, he teaches that the confession that 'Christ has come in the flesh' is the work and mark of the true Spirit against any and all false spirits (1 John 4:2,3). The Apostles and the Early Church knew of many spirits (see 1 Tim. 4:2,3), but they knew one sure test which could be used to distinguish between such and the Spirit. They knew that it was only the Spirit of Christ who could testify to Christ and produce faith in Him (Rev. 19:10; see also 1 John 4:6 and 5:5,6).

All this is the necessary background for a correct understanding of those strange words of Paul in 2 Cor. 3:17,18: 'Now the Lord is the Spirit, and where the Spirit of the Lord is, there is freedom'. The apostle did not mean to confuse the persons of the Son and the Spirit, but rather sought to impress on his readers the inseparability of both persons in the work of salvation. The Spirit dare not be divorced from Jesus Christ. Consequently, the preaching of a different Jesus or the reception of a different Spirit, than the Jesus and the Spirit which Paul knows, means the reception of a different gospel which is no gospel at all (2 Cor. 11:4)!

Jesus has left one 'last will and testament' to His church, and the executor of that will is the Spirit.

2. The word *pneuma*, referring to the Holy Spirit, occurs some 32 times in Paul's letter to the Romans, but of these occurrences we find 20 in Romans 8! This is the chapter in which Paul climaxed his argument on justification by faith alone in terms of the present reality and assurance of salvation for the believer. It is here that the full significance of the contrast between the 'law [= norm] of the Spirit of life in Jesus Christ' and the 'law of sin and death' is drawn out (Rom. 8:2). It is only those who walk by faith who fulfil the law. Verse 9 again gives us the equation which we deduced earlier from Galatians: having the Spirit of Christ = being a Christian:

> 'But you are not in the flesh [that is, under the condemning power of sin], you are in the Spirit, if the Spirit of God really dwells in you. Any one who does not have the Spirit of Christ does not belong to him.'

The conditional clause, 'if the Spirit really dwells in you', is not meant to raise doubts in the minds of the Roman Christians that they have the Spirit, but is meant to remind them of what they most assuredly are and have: 'you are in the Spirit'! Paul is reminding them of the significance of this possession. There can, indeed, be a **limited rule of the Spirit** (where the believer does not allow the Spirit to lead him as he should), but there is **no part-possession of the Spirit**. The same Spirit who raised Jesus from the dead (v. 11; see also Rom. 1:4; 1 Tim. 3:16; 1 Peter 3:18,19) has raised the believer to a new life, and lives in him to fight the battle against the 'flesh'.

Pentecostals make a great deal of sanctification as a precondition for a full reception of the Spirit. But this is putting the cart before the horse. Any sanctification at all is possible only through the very possession of Christ's Spirit. We shall return to the question of sanctification presently; for the moment we shall briefly note two further points, both of which show that every Christian possesses the Spirit in all His fullness.

3. Both in Romans and Galatians, Paul stresses the inseparability of faith and the Spirit. The 'full assurance of faith' is the first and most important fruit of the Spirit (Col. 2:2,5). Since He is the creator of faith, the Spirit is constantly mentioned together with faith (as in Acts 6:5 and 11:24). He is indeed 'the spirit of faith' (2 Cor. 4:13). But this faith is not mere knowledge about the existence of God, but confident trust in Him as Father, the confidence that in Christ we 'have access in one Spirit to the Father' (Eph. 2:18). We have already seen how Paul and John trace the very confession to the incarnate and glorified Christ back to the work of the Spirit; Paul goes one step further when he says that the very cry of the believer to God of 'Abba! Father!' is the 'Spirit himself bearing witness with our spirit that we are children of God, and if children then heirs . . .' (Rom. 8:15,16).

In an almost direct parallel in Galatians, Paul writes: 'God sent forth his Son . . . that we might receive adoption as sons. And because you are sons, God has sent the Spirit of his Son into our hearts, crying "Abba! Father!"' (Gal. 4:4–6). Verse 6, with its 'because you are sons, God has sent the Spirit', does not mean that believers are first declared to be God's children and only subsequently given the Spirit. This is made impossible by Romans 8 where believers are made sons by the Spirit who is given to all believers. The 'because' clause suggests not a condition for reception, but the very fact of reception itself. Paul is saying: Those who are God's children have the Spirit, and therefore can call God Father. All Christians, not just a few who claim 'a second experience of the Spirit', are therefore addressed as 'spiritual' (*pneumatikoi*) in Gal. 6:1.

4. What Paul calls 'adoption as sons/children' (*hyiothesia*) is another way of expressing the present possession of salvation. Believers who are led by the Spirit are already now sons of God (Rom. 8:14). And yet they 'wait for adoption as sons' (v. 23). This is no contradiction, but another expression of the twofold truth and tension in which the Christian lives. He is both sinner and saint; he has salvation and waits for salvation. He believes, but still hopes. It is the Spirit who gives both faith and hope (Eph. 4:4), who leads us through the tension of having and not having.

Faith and the assurance of the present possession of a right relationship with God is the 'first fruit of the Spirit' (Rom. 8:23), but the same Spirit makes us long for the fulfilment and perfecting of all God's promises in Christ. Not only believers but the whole of creation longs for this fulfilment (vv. 18–27). By the power of the Spirit we 'abound in hope' (Rom. 15:13).

Paul uses two terms for the Spirit to enforce this point: He is the 'seal' and 'guarantee' of salvation. In 2 Cor. 1:15–24 Paul answers the accusation of the Corinthians that he is not a man of his word. They seem to be saying: Paul is always talking about visiting us, but never gets here! In reply he protests his own trustworthiness as an apostle of the Lord, as one who speaks the truth of God whose faithfulness has been demonstrated once and for all in Jesus Christ. God's fidelity is seen in his dealing with Paul and his readers:

> 'It is God who establishes us with you in Christ, and has commissioned us; he has put his seal upon us and given us his Spirit in our hearts as a guarantee' (2 Cor. 1:21,22).

The three verbs, 'commissioned' (really the word means 'anointed'), 'sealed', and 'given', all point to an event in the past, and must refer again to the original experience of grace itself. Paul's point about Christian assurance would be lost if only a few of his readers had been anointed and sealed with the Spirit! Barnett and Jensen (*The Quest for Power*, p. 47) rightly suggest that 'anointed' or 'christed' really is a reference to being baptized into the body of Christ, the church.

The word for 'guarantee' (*arrabon*) is used by Paul as a description of the Spirit also in 2 Cor. 5:5 and Eph. 1:13,14. The word, which means a down payment or deposit which guarantees a full future settlement of an account, is always used in the context of Christian hope. But, far from suggesting a future full possession of the Spirit, it denotes the present full possession of the Spirit as the basis of hope itself.

'Sealing' suggests another picture, the stamp on a document or some other object which certifies it as genuine or as under specific ownership. The three occasions where Paul uses the verb in connection with the Spirit (2 Cor. 1:22; Eph. 1:13; 4:30) suggest the image of the Spirit as God's personal stamp or seal on the believer which marks him as God's for all eternity.

Once more the doctrine of subsequence fails the biblical test. One of the most obvious conclusions from the passages which speak of the Spirit as seal and guarantee is that the Spirit comes from the hearing of faith, as in Gal. 3:2. Thus Eph. 1:13,14 links the hearing of the Word, faith, and the sealing with the Spirit, as one event.

If we make the gift of the Spirit some 'extra', over and above the experience of salvation and coming to faith in the first place, we do not only misunderstand a few isolated passages in Scripture; we detract from the certainty of salvation itself. Christian faith and hope are both the 'fruit of the Spirit' (note how Paul uses the singular 'fruit', not the plural, in Gal. 5:22). The work of the Spirit in raising the Son from the dead, in giving us new life in the Son, is the guarantee that we will also share in the promised resurrection where we will be given spiritual bodies (1 Cor. 15:44–46). Even at the last, the Spirit promises to give us what is the Son's, eternal life and glory with the Father (1 Peter 4:14; Gal. 5:5).

3. 'Be Filled with the Spirit'—The Call to Holiness

In his explanation to the Third Article of the Apostles' Creed, Dr. Martin Luther has taught us to confess that the Spirit not only calls, gathers, and enlightens, but also sanctifies Christ's church. The New Testament uses the term 'sanctify' in various ways. Basic to the word is the idea of setting something or someone apart as holy. For example, in the Old Testament, men or objects were holy insofar as they were set apart for special use in the service of God, or marked as God's possession. Holiness in its original meaning does not denote moral purity. Thus the Spirit's work in sanctifying believers is part of, or an aspect of, the work of salvation itself. 'God chose you from the beginning to be saved, through sanctification by the Spirit and belief in the truth' (2 Thess. 2:13); or, as Peter puts it: God's saints are those who have been 'sanctified by the Spirit for obedience [of faith] to Jesus Christ and for sprinkling with his blood' (1 Peter 1:2). In this sense, the Gentiles also have been 'sanctified by the Holy Spirit' (Rom. 15:16). To reject salvation is thus to outrage the Spirit (Heb. 10:29).

We know that this great act of setting sinners apart as saints of God takes place wherever and whenever men accept their justification by God's act in Jesus, and His free offer of grace in Christ, accepted by faith alone. But this gift is, in turn, the basis of the call to holiness and of the actual life of sanctification. God's verdict, 'I declare you just in my Son', is not just a declaration of a wonderful truth; it is the gift of grace as the divine power which sets to work in the believer to lead him to live a life that corresponds to his new being.

The call to holiness is thus a call to submit to the rule of the Spirit who has been given to the believer. And so Paul issues the challenge: 'God has not called us for uncleanness, but in holiness. Therefore whoever disregards this, disregards not man but God, who gives his Spirit to us' (1 Thess. 4:7,8; see James 4:5). God's saints are renewed also in the spirit of their minds (Eph. 4:23)—in order to live the new life that is from start to finish the gift of the Spirit. Holiness is not human works, but a matter of letting the Holy Spirit stamp us as what we are: God's different people.

While we have refuted the charismatic doctrine of the baptism of the Spirit, we have not taken up so far the one passage in Paul's letters which contains **the call to be filled with the Spirit** (Eph. 5:18). Must we now do some back-tracking, and admit that there is a second experience of the Spirit? A careful look at the exact grammar of this verse and its context must lead us to answer again in the negative.

We note, first of all, that this verse stands in a long section of exhortations to holiness, more particularly, in a section which calls readers to 'walk as children of light' (5:8). This appeal presupposes that they **are already** in the light (the truth of the Gospel). Likewise, the appeal to be filled with the Spirit presupposes that they **already have** the Spirit. The form of the verb (an imperative in the continuous present tense) allows a number of translations such as: 'Be continuously filled with the Spirit', 'Stay filled with the Spirit'. There is simply no suggestion that they must now seek a filling of the Spirit for the first time.

Secondly, the signs of the Spirit's presence in the believers should be noted carefully. There is no mention here of spectacular, supernatural manifestations of the Spirit. His presence comes to the fore in what we call the priesthood of all believers, in singing praise and thanks to God, and in encouraging others. The most direct parallel to this passage, Col. 3:15–17, gives us the same picture of the Spirit at work in the church. Those who have been called into one body, who have been baptized into Christ (Col. 2:12), are called to sing 'Spirit-worked songs', to let the Spirit lead them to sing the glorious doxology of God and His work in Christ. The Spirit is there where there is praise of God! But that is not held out merely as a distant ideal, as a remote possibility in the future after they have received a special filling of the Spirit; this is what can be expected of every baptized Christian who believes the Gospel and has the Spirit of Christ within him. Paul knows no higher second experience of the Spirit.

Being filled with the Spirit certainly means being led on to a new life of holiness. St. Paul expresses the struggle for holiness as the fight of the Spirit against the written code of the Law which kills as it condemns, yes, which even eggs man on to sin insofar as it invites disobedience, or bolsters up human pride and self-sufficiency (Rom. 7:7–12). This is a struggle against death itself. By accepting the gift of forgiveness in Christ, the sinner has been freed from the curse of the Law which he could never keep perfectly, and freed to live 'in the new life of the Spirit' (Rom. 7:6). 'The written code kills, but the Spirit gives life' (2 Cor. 3:6) shows that the Spirit is the equivalent of new life in the Gospel as opposed to the old life under the Law. If the Law is removed as a basis for holiness, then man as 'flesh' (as sinner in the totality of his being) no longer has a leg to stand on—unless he accepts God's free gift of holiness, first declared as a gift in Christ, and then worked out in practical terms in the believer's life by the power of the Spirit. The only holiness acceptable to God is the new life lived in the Spirit. And so Paul contrasts the old life lived to the flesh with the new life of the Spirit (Rom. 8:2–13).

Several other observations underline the truth that the whole of the believer's life as a life of holiness (= sanctification) is the work of the Spirit, and thus presupposes the prior indwelling of the Spirit in the first place.

Paul's call to live a new life is **baptismal** exhortation. While this is not always explicit in many texts, it is quite clearly the case in Romans 6. Baptism into Christ is baptism into His death. But the fruit of that union is also a being raised to 'newness of life' (Rom. 6:1–5) since we are also united with the **risen** Lord. Baptism not only marks the believer as one who is under **new ownership**, under the lordship of Christ. He is now also under **new management**, insofar as he is 'led by the Spirit' (Rom. 8:14). Holiness is thus a walking or living 'according to the Spirit' (8:4,5), which corresponds to the new life given in Baptism. While justification and sanctification must not be confused, they must also never be separated, for the second flows from the first. They form a unity with the Spirit as the power behind both.

That holiness is actually a submitting to a new power in one's life is made clear in two passages to which we can briefly refer. Romans 6 not only pictures the new life in Christ and the Spirit as a gift in Baptism; it also pictures holiness as a matter of 'yielding oneself'. No man is master of himself; he is the slave either of sin or of righteousness. While Paul speaks of yielding to God, or yielding to righteousness (vv. 13 and 19), Romans 8 shows that he could also speak of yielding to the Holy Spirit. Thus, if justification by faith means to 'let God be God [the God of grace]', sanctification means to 'let the Spirit be the Spirit [the Spirit of holiness]'!

Gal. 5:16–25 is perhaps an even more compressed and powerful statement of the point just stated. Once more Paul speaks of 'walking by the Spirit' or being 'led by the Spirit' as the great contrast to walking according to the flesh (vv. 16,18,25). We should note several points in order to appreciate this contrast fully.

a) Flesh and Spirit are diametrically opposed. While 'flesh' describes man in his totality as sinner, and the power of sin itself within man, 'Spirit' denotes the power of God, which is not man's natural possession, not a higher principle within man, but an external power. He comes to man, not from within him. Flesh and Spirit are thus not two parts or aspects of man himself.

b) What flesh is becomes dear in Paul's catalogue of sins in vv. 19–21. It is not an abstract principle, but a power which has its own concrete 'works'. The flesh is not identified only with certain obviously carnal sins like sexual licence, gluttony, and drunkenness. It is seen in all those sins which arise from man's self assertive ego, and in all idolatry, as man attempts to make and serve his own gods.

c) In contrast to the works (plural) of the flesh, Paul lists the fruit (singular) of the Spirit (v. 22). The Christian life is not a collection of individual virtues, as in Hellenistic moral philosophy, but a unity. Love, joy, peace, patience, kindness, goodness, faithfulness, gentleness, self-control, and the like, are not man-produced works, but the Spirit-produced fruit.

d) Not only is the fruit of the Spirit a unity; faith and life as the work of the Spirit also constitute a unity. 'If we live by the Spirit, let us also walk by the Spirit' (v. 25). The first clause describes the new being in the Spirit, a new existence in faith; the second describes the new life by the power of the Spirit. The second presupposes the first; any attempt to make the reception of the Spirit dependent on a later full reception of the Spirit again puts the cart before the horse.

Life according to the Spirit is not a new existence which lifts the believer out of the ever-present reality of sin. The teaching of Paul that the believer is sinner and saint at the same time, that he is always under the total Word of God (both the Law which condemns and the Gospel which saves) clearly disallows any perfectionism. Where the believer is indeed led by the Spirit, there will be growth as the Spirit is allowed to overcome the power of sin in the 'flesh'. But any suggestion that the Christian can reach the point where sin is no longer a power, where perfect holiness is reached, fails to understand the nature and power of sin, as well as the continual validity of the Law. As Melanchthon, Luther's friend and ally, said: *Lex semper accusat* (the Law always accuses). We escape its **damning** accusation only as long as we are covered by the Gospel, accepted in faith. We emphasize this since Pentecostalism has grown out of the holiness-movement which stressed sanctification itself as the second blessing of the Spirit, and which often ended up with a completely unbiblical perfectionism.

On the other hand, charismatics are correct when they emphasize the call to holiness as a call to submit to the Spirit, and suggest that this emphasis is often missing in the churches. It is all very well to have a correct doctrine of the Spirit, but where life does not reflect faith, one can rightly suspect that the Spirit's path is being blocked. The fact that the Spirit dwells in our very bodies (1 Cor. 6:19; 2 Tim. 1:14; James 4:5) means that there is no area of human life in which the Christian can escape the call to holiness. While it is true that the holiness of a believer is never the final proof of his being saved, the least that one can expect from him is a life that will seek to glorify God and His Son in everything that he does. To be a spiritual person means to be directed by the Holy Spirit.

One final point on the Spirit and the spiritual life. If believers have received Christ and His Spirit, then the whole parcel of God's good gifts are handed over to His children. We have noted that this 'parcel' is a unity, the fruit of the Spirit; it is the natural by-product of being possessed by the Spirit of Christ. We have a listing of these good gifts not only in Gal. 5:22,23; similar lists are found elsewhere: 'righteousness and peace and joy in the Holy Spirit' (Rom. 14:17); 'joy and peace . . . hope' (Rom. 15:13); 'love and self-control' (2 Tim. 1:7); and individual 'fruits' are mentioned' in Gal. 6:1 (gentleness) and 1 Thess. 1:6 (joy). This list is, of course, not complete, since it only cites those passages which contain a mention of the Spirit. While it is clear that faith, hope, and love are the chief fruit of the Spirit (1 Thess. 1:3; Col. 1:4,5; 1 Cor. 13:13), and that the fruit of the Spirit can never be separated from the gift of salvation itself, the one fruit that is stressed in the Christian life is love.

The church is a fellowship or community of love in the Spirit, for 'God's love has been poured into our hearts through the Holy Spirit which has been given to us' (Rom. 5:5). Here again the Spirit does nothing more than give the gift of Christ Himself, who gave the command: 'Abide in my love' (John 15:9). Because the experience of God's love is synonymous with the experience of salvation itself, love, like faith and hope, is the common possession of all believers, and that to which the apostle can appeal as a basis for right ethical behaviour (Rom. 15:30; Col. 1:8). Love can, indeed, be seen as the foundation of the fellowship in the Spirit (2 Cor. 13:14; Phil. 2:1).

But it is important to note how love as the fulfilling of the law (Rom. 13:8,10), as faith in action (Gal. 5:6), is the real mark of the spiritual life as the life of holiness. It is important to note this, because, whether correctly or not, one gains the impression that charismatic piety is sometimes a flight into the non-material world, into an other-worldliness which bypasses the ethic of love. True spirituality in the New Testament is something very concrete, physical, even mundane! Rom. 12:1,2 shows that holiness means a complete change of thinking and attitudes, a transformation of the mind. But the way in which this is expressed is a surrendering of one's body as a spiritual sacrifice. This does not mean a negative ethic, one filled with prohibitions of all the things one should not do, but a positive giving of oneself for the fellow-man. The Christian is called to live 'theologically', that is, to live a life of worship in the praise of God. But love for God is expressed in practical service to fellow-human beings. A spirituality that escapes from the tangible, practical, material obligations of service in every-day existence into an other-worldly communing with God, into religious experience, yes, even into acts of worship, praise, and prayer alone, is no true spirituality. Worship and prayer are, indeed, the province of the Spirit (Rom. 2:29; 8:26,27; Eph. 6:18; Phil. 1:19; 3:3), but they are the beginning, not the end of the spiritual life.

That a piety of attitude without action is a danger not limited to charismatic circles, but found among all Christians, hardly needs stating!

4. The Spirit and the Spectacular

Charismatics are most often identified with the claim to possess spectacular signs of the Spirit's presence, especially speaking in tongues, prophecy, and faith-healing. While this is an oversimplification of their position, it is true that they stress the power of the Spirit to work the same signs and wonders as in New Testament times. Further, the chief result of the second experience of the Spirit is seen as 'power for witness'. What is the truth in regard to the Spirit and such power?

1. The word *dynamis* (power) is certainly used in the New Testament as a description of the Spirit. He is God's dynamo! Jesus promised His disciples 'power when the Holy Spirit has come upon you; and you shall be my witnesses . . .' (Acts 1:8). The couplet 'Spirit and power' (Luke 1:17; Acts 10:38; 1 Cor. 2:4; Eph. 3:16; 1 Thess. 1:5) or the phrase 'power of the Holy Spirit' (Luke 4:14; Rom. 15:13,19) show that *dynamis* is often simply a synonym for the Spirit Himself (see Luke 1:35).

2. We note that the Spirit did indeed give the apostles power for witness. The key-word used in Acts to describe the transformed attitude of the disciples after Pentecost is *parrhesia* (boldness; Acts 2:29; 4:13,29–31; the related verb appears in 9:27,28; 13:46; 14:3; 18:26; 19:8; 26:26). Whereas they had earlier been huddled together like frightened rabbits in some Jerusalem attic (Acts 1:13), they now went out to face the whole world and claim it for Christ! Only the gift of the Spirit can explain this utter transformation.

3. Just as Jesus' preaching had been accompanied by miracles (Acts 2:22; 10:38), so the apostles work miracles in the name of Jesus and by the power of the

Spirit. It is the power of Jesus' name which figures most prominently in Acts, not the power of the Spirit. But this distinction is not important when we remember that the Spirit is the **Spirit of Jesus**. Like Jesus, Peter and Paul heal the lame (Acts 3:1–10; 14:8–14), raise the dead (9:40,41; 20:10), and drive out demons (5:16; 16:16–18). The Spirit of prophecy was again active in the Early Church, as seen from the example of Agabus and the four unmarried daughters of Philip (Acts 11:27,28; 21:8–11). Furthermore, Gal. 3:5 reflects the fact that the coming of the Spirit with the hearing of the Gospel was still accompanied by signs (see also Rom. 15:19 and Heb. 2:4).

All this seems to substantiate the claim that the Spirit is power for witness, and the one who works miracles to accompany that witness. Is there, then, any good reason why these signs and this power should not be present for all to see in the church today? We shall look at specific charismatic gifts in the next section; for the moment we shall examine more closely the New Testament understanding of power and the work of the Spirit.

One thing must be said as clearly and emphatically as possible from the outset: **the apostolic Word, the preaching of the Gospel, is that place where the power of the Spirit is seen at work and experienced by the believer**. The Spirit's power is also seen in spectacular signs or in the renewed life of holiness, but the Word remains the Spirit's base of operation. In the above statement there are two words which require amplification: "word' and 'apostolic'.

1. In the age of the New Testament, the Spirit did, and continues to do now, what Jesus had promised: 'He will take what is mine and **declare** it to you' (John 16:14). The apostles testified that the Old Testament writers already witnessed to Christ and the salvation that was to be offered in Him (Heb. 3:7; 9:8; 10:15–17; 1 Peter 1:11; 2 Peter 1:21). They, as authorized agents of the risen Lord (i.e. apostles), claimed to speak the truth of this salvation by the power of the same Spirit. Actually, they rather seldom made an **explicit** claim to be speaking by the Spirit (Rom. 9:1; 1 Cor. 7:40; 14:37; 2 Cor. 6:6; 12:18; Rev. 1:10; 4:2; 17:3); however, the claim that they spoke by the Spirit was **implied** at every turn (see also Eph. 3:5).

The Spirit worked signs through the apostles, but that which produced faith was their humble word which was accepted 'not as the word of men but as what it really is, the word of God' (1 Thess. 2:13). Paul recalled in Rom. 15:18–20 how his now-completed mission in the eastern world had included 'word and deed'; Christ had been at work in him 'by the power of signs and wonders, by the power of the Holy Spirit'. But the Spirit's power was seen, first and foremost, in his preaching of the Gospel, not in miracles (v. 20).

To the Corinthians, who had come to despise the humble preaching of the cross in the pursuit of a higher wisdom, Paul said: 'When I came to you . . . my speech and my message were not in plausible words of wisdom, but in demonstration of the Spirit and power' (1 Cor. 2:1–4). The Gospel, the humble preaching of a shameful cross, remains the power of God (1 Cor. 1:18,24). If there were any faith and understanding among the Corinthians, it was not because of their power or wisdom (1:26–31), not because of Paul's own wisdom or eloquence (2:1–5), but because the great Enlightener, the Spirit of God, had been at work among them in the message they had heard. Man as flesh is not able to receive the things of God unless he first receives the Spirit (2:14; 3:1; John 3:6; Eph. 1:17). The apostles preached with full conviction, but it was the Spirit who gave their words the **power of conviction** (1 Thess. 1:5; 1 Peter 1:12). The Word of God, also where it is preached by men today, is the 'sword of the Spirit' (Eph. 6:17).

The apostles went out 'demanding' faith in Christ, not faith in or through signs and wonders. These only 'attended' the Word. The signs of the Spirit's presence and the assurance of salvation were seen in the 'fruit' of His work, in the lives of the believers themselves. And it was the Gospel through which the Spirit produced His fruit (Col. 1:6,8).

'He who believes and is baptized will be saved' is the promise of Mark 16:16. God's child knows with absolute certainty that he is saved; he does not have to look beyond the promise itself for further proof. Faith does not become sure by experiential or empirical verification. It has its own sure anchor in the faithfulness of God to His promises (Rom. 3:3,4).

2. Paul's defence of his apostolate in **2 Corinthians** can be seen as his most powerful statement on the preaching of the Cross as the power of God. It has been argued by critics of the apostle that Paul was obsessed with his own self-importance, with his own personal dignity and authority. Quite clearly the Corinthians (or some of them) had questioned his apostolic authority. After all, that was to some extent only to be expected, since Paul did not belong to the original eyewitnesses of the risen Lord. But Paul is not interested in saving face for himself. Indeed, in this letter he deliberately plays the fool and argues like a mad man (2 Cor. 11:1,21,23)! It was Christ who called him to be an apostle (1 Cor. 9:1; 15:8–11); it was from Christ that he received the Gospel (Gal. 1:12). Thus in defending his apostleship he was doing nothing more than defending Christ and the Gospel itself.

The Spirit assumed a central position in the argument regarding the criteria by which a genuine apostle was to be judged. Paul had to fight for the recognition of his ministry as a ministry of the Spirit (2 Cor. 3:6–8). He had been challenged to prove that he had the Spirit by those who claimed the Spirit for themselves and for some pseudo-apostles. They missed the 'signs of an apostle' in Paul; they missed the obvious certification of the Spirit with signs of power (10:10).

Paul's answer is nothing short of amazing. Although 'there is nothing to be gained by it' (2 Cor. 12:1), Paul cites his visions and revelations, his supernatural ecstatic experiences as evidence that he has the Spirit. But, instead of boasting about these, he recalls the 'thorn in the flesh' which the Lord had not removed despite the apostle's frequent pleas (v. 7). He refuses to boast of power, and instead boasts of his weakness (4:7–10; 10:30; 12:5,9)! He also reminds his readers that 'the signs of a true apostle were performed among you in all patience, with signs and wonders and mighty works' (12:12). But not even these are used to prove that he has the Spirit or that the Spirit has been at work through him. No, instead he recalls his long sufferings for the Lord (6:4–10; 11:21–33; 12:10). If they want the one proof of the Spirit, 'proof that Christ is speaking in me', they should look to his preaching of the Lord who was 'crucified in weakness, but lives by the power of God' (13:3,4). To say it again quite simply: the proof of the Spirit's power lies not in spectacular signs, but in the preaching of the Cross as it produces faith.

Paul rejected any theology of glory that takes us beyond the Cross as the demonstration of divine power, beyond our continual dependence on the grace offered there. God's power is made perfect in our weakness, and that is the only boasting we can ever do. If our witness becomes 'power', it is not because of something in us, but because of something in the witness itself, the dynamo of the Spirit.

3. The concept of power in the New Testament was linked with the apostles as the original eyewitnesses of the Lord. Where power was linked with all believers, it was power not for witness but for godly living (although a holy life is, of course, the first great witness the believer can give to others). This is the power of Christ's own resurrection-life (Eph. 1:19; 3:16,20; Phil. 3:10; Col. 1:11). Nowhere in the entire New Testament do we find a special gift of the Spirit apart from conversion itself with power for witness. The two instances in Acts where there is testimony to Christ after the reception of the Spirit (2:14 and 9:20) picture the **apostles** proclaiming Christ. The special outpourings of the Spirit at Samaria, Caesarea, and Ephesus do not mention any subsequent witnessing with power on the part of the Samaritans, Cornelius, or the Ephesian Christians.

Why link power with the apostles in this way? All four Gospels (especially the Fourth) picture Jesus' ministry as a ministry of word and deed. Jesus' miracles, whether healings or exorcisms, were to be seen as evidence that the Messianic age had arrived. His miracles were not bits of magic or entertainment (a bit of hocus-pocus to impress or amuse the crowd); they were themselves the Gospel in action; they were acted illustrations of the message of God's forgiving love and mercy.

Miracles also figure in the ministry of Jesus' apostles. While the title of apostle was given in the Early Church to others than the original Twelve, to men whom we might call 'missionaries' (see Acts 14:4,14 and 1 Cor. 15:7), the word 'apostle' in the strict sense meant one who had been personally authorized, commissioned, and sent by the risen Lord Himself. Thus the office of the apostle was unique in the church in that it disappeared in time. The apostles could not appoint other apostles; they could only leave behind spiritual leaders who would continue to preach the truth they had preached and taught. Thus it was understandable and really to be expected that the chosen apostles of Jesus should have the power to carry on the same works that He did. But there was no absolute promise that these miracles would continue for all ages in the church.

4. There are especially three passages which are used from time to time to prove that Jesus promised that there would always be signs accompanying the preaching of the Word. The first is John 14:12, where Jesus says:

> 'Truly, truly, I say to you, he who believes in me will also do the works that I do; and greater works than these will he do, because I go to the Father'.

The reference to His going to the Father can be linked with Jesus' earlier promise to send the Spirit after His glorification (John 7:39); for the above text is immediately followed by the first promise of the Paraclete (14:15–17). Certainly, the 'greater works' are not promised only to the disciples to whom He spoke these words; the promise applies to everyone 'who believes in me'. But the Church Fathers, as well as commentators in our day, are generally agreed that the works here promised are not miracles in the sense of spectacular signs, but the miracles of conversion. None of the five Paraclete-sayings speaks of deeds in the sense of signs—Jesus is the only one who can work a true *semeion* (sign) in the sense of John's Gospel—but they do promise that the Spirit will lead disciples of all ages into the truth of the Gospel.

The second text to be considered is the promise of signs in v. 17,18 of the longer ending of **Mark's Gospel [16:9–20]**. The first thing to be said here is that it is unwise to base any argument on this passage alone. (We have used Mark 16:16 elsewhere only because it teaches a truth that clearly permeates the whole New Testament.) On the basis of careful studies, and without any bias against what the verses contain, scholars have repeatedly shown that this longer ending to Mark is a secondary source. There is no need here to give any of the scholarly arguments against the primary authenticity and originality of the passage; the brief summaries offered by Barnett and Jensen (*The Quest for Power*, pp. 81,82) and Hoekema (*What about Tongue Speaking?*, pp. 53–56) are quite accurate and adequate for those who are interested.

But, even if the passage were original, there are still problems. If the Pentecostal argues from this passage the necessity of the miracles of tongues, exorcisms, and healings in our day, why not also insist on the other promises that believers will handle snakes and drink poison without being harmed? At least there are some Pentecostals who are completely consistent at this point; the American Church of Signs Following does indeed feature snake-handling and the drinking of poison as proofs of the Spirit—with some very sad and fatal results!

Finally, **1 Cor. 12:28** is also used to prove the permanence of the miraculous in the church.

> 'And God has appointed in the church first apostles, second prophets, third teachers, then workers of miracles, then healers, helpers, administrators, speakers in various kinds of tongues.'

Lest we be misunderstood, let it be made clear that we are not denying that miracles can take place today; we are denying that the New Testament promises that they will and must take place in all subsequent times. The above text makes no such promise.

It cannot be pressed into service as a text which speaks of God's permanent activity in the church, since there is clearly one gift mentioned that certainly lapsed in the church—the gift of the apostleship.

5. It would probably be helpful at this point to marshal some reasons why signs and wonders were very much a part of the apostolic church. First, we have noted how the apostles were the follow-on agents of the risen Lord whose ministry had been one of word and deed. Secondly, the New Testament church as yet had no New Testament canon which they could cite as the authoritative Word of God and the basis for Christian faith and life. Certainly there were living witnesses, the apostles, but there were also pseudo-apostles, as the Galatian and Corinthian Letters show. In this situation, the need for special signs of the Spirit to accompany the preaching of the Word can be readily understood. Thirdly, one can say that the miraculous is commonplace in New Testament times. The rabbis are reported to have worked miracles, and there were also plenty of Hellenistic miracle-workers. It would have been very strange, indeed, for a new faith to appear on that world-scene without any supernatural signs. The point at issue is not whether the signs claimed for other miracle-workers were genuine miracles. The point is that the miraculous was simply an accepted part of people's thinking in that day.

Our argument, then, is simply this: one can neither prove nor disprove from the New Testament that miracles are to continue in the church through all ages; what we can do is to put the miraculous and the spectacular in right perspective. Miracles in the New Testament serve the proclamation of the Word. The miraculous is itself always open to interpretation. Its message must be gathered from the Word, not from itself. It bears saying again that even the demonic can produce signs (Matt. 7:22,23; 24:24).

We must say this since Pentecostalism shows a preoccupation with signs and spectacular demonstrations of spiritual power, as the advertisements in our daily papers publicizing Pentecostal services and meetings clearly indicate. Neo-Pentecostals lay themselves open to the charge from time to time that they, too, suffer from a distorted evaluation of external signs of the Spirit. To them we also say again: the great miracle is salvation itself, the miracle of grace, the miracle that takes place when a person comes to faith.

6. Barnett and Jensen have rightly warned against a craving for personal power. Power, in the New Testament, never belongs to man; it belongs to God, to the Gospel, to the Spirit. God only uses human weakness to demonstrate His divine power.

The wrong understanding of power largely rests on a false anthropology, a wrong understanding of man. In *The Holy Spirit and You: A Study-Guide to the Spirit-Filled Life*, the American Episcopalian charismatics, Dennis and Rita Bennett, argue that man is a 'threefold being: spirit, soul and body', citing 1 Thess. 5:23. They polemicize against a two-part division of man into only body and soul:

> 'When you received Jesus as your Saviour, your spirit came alive, began to assert its new life and take its rightful place as head over your

> soul—your psychological part (intellect, will and emotions)—and your body, your physical part' (see pp. 17 and 35).

Although the anthropological argument is very unclear, the idea seems to be that the Spirit first renews man's spirit, as some part of man, and then through the spirit gains mastery of the whole person. With this argument one can understand how the gift of the Spirit becomes identified with the internal possession of power for witness. Power becomes the internal possession of the man's spirit. This position is rejected because of the following points:

1. In the New Testament, man is neither of two parts (dichotomous) nor of three parts (trichotomous). He does not have spirit, soul, body, flesh; he is all these. Each of these terms describes man from a different aspect. And some of the terms are interchangeable; one cannot always make a clear distinction between spirit and soul, or between flesh and body.
2. Man's spirit is not that part of man which is closer to God than any other part, nor that part of man which has a closer affinity to the Spirit. Man's spirit can, theologically speaking, also be called 'flesh'.
3. The **whole person** is renewed by the Spirit, not just a part of him. The redeemed person is, and remains, a unity, a totality. As we have pointed out, man's body is just as involved with the Spirit as his 'spirit' or 'soul'.
4. Divine power is never made part of man himself, either in Paul or in any other part of the New Testament. God remains God and man remains man, even if Christ and His Spirit come to live in the believer. There is no mixing of the divine and human such as we find in Hellenistic mysticism, where the person who had his spiritual experience in an initiation ceremony in a mystery-cult could be hailed as 'divine'.

Power never belongs to man. It belongs to God as Paul clearly states: 'The transcendent power belongs to God and not to us'; God's 'power is made perfect in weakness' (2 Cor. 4:7 and 12:9). All the statements in Scripture which speak of Christ as 'the power of God' (1 Cor. 1:24), or of the Spirit or the Gospel as God's power, only develop the point that power belongs to God. Where this is not confessed, the Christian who receives some special spiritual experience and some charismatic gift can all too easily fall into the temptation to enjoy an 'ego trip', a wonderful feeling of power vested in him/herself. That temptation is as real for the charismatic as it is for the pastor who can mount his pulpit and enjoy the feeling of power which he has over all the people seated below him.

5. The Charismatic Gifts and Ministry

Paul's teaching on the gifts of the Spirit in 1 Corinthians 12–14 must be seen: within the context of the whole Letter and the problems at Corinth which can be deduced from it. By reading these chapters in their context, much that is said about charismatic gifts, about tongues in particular, is soon seen to be untenable. The important thing is not that Paul says there is a gift of tongues; the vital question is: What is the importance and place of this gift, and other gifts, within the individual life of faith, and what is its function within the body of Christ?

Although about half of the occurrences of *pneuma* in 1 Corinthians occur in chapters 12 and 14, we should not forget the great stress on the Spirit in the early chapters, especially 1–3. We have seen how Paul had to fight against any addition to, or subtraction from, the Gospel. Against the 'spirituals' (*pneumatikoi*), Paul pleads for a return to the theology of the Cross. The Gospel is not some special human wisdom or *gnosis* ('knowledge'), or some spectacular sign; it remains the message of a shameful death on a cross; it is the story of God's seeming weakness and folly (1 Cor. 1:18–25). Of course, it has its own power, but the power of the Gospel is the Spirit of God who uses the preaching of the Cross to save man. The repeated mention of the Cross or Christ crucified is a sure indication that the Corinthians would have liked to escape from the offence of history into a gospel turned into a timeless myth.

For Greek thinking, truth did not belong to this world, which is only a shadow of the other, real world of ideas (Plato). Thus early Gnosticism, under Hellenistic influences, taught a higher 'knowledge' (*gnosis*) which went far beyond simple 'faith' (*pistis*); truth was a matter of special revelation and wisdom which was not necessarily bound to an historical person, Jesus of Nazareth, and what happened to Him on a cross. The New Testament writers had to fight this de-historicizing process at various points. Recall the warning against what was 'falsely called knowledge' (*gnosis*) in 1 Tim. 6:20, and the insistence that Christ had come in the flesh in John 1:14 and 1 John 4:2. In the later, fully-developed Gnostic systems of the second century, we find a confessing of Christ which bypassed the Jesus of history. It has thus been suggested, with some justification, that the confession '**Jesus** is Lord' in 1 Cor. 12:3 is a subtle polemic against those in Corinth who eagerly confessed the glorified Christ but rejected all this talk about a crucified Jesus. Consequently, some have seen the slogan 'I belong to Christ' in 1:12 as that which belonged to a separate party in Corinth. Be that as it may, the Corinthian enthusiasts not only claimed the Spirit, but through this Spirit claimed special knowledge above faith. But Paul will hear of no knowledge that is not at the same time faith in the crucified Lord (1:17,18,23; 2:2,8).

All the various moral abuses at Corinth can likewise be understood against the background of a special spiritual enthusiasm. The Corinthians are so 'spiritual' that they have as their catch-cry 'All things are lawful for me' (6:12; 10:23). They also claim special knowledge (*gnosis*), according to the slogan cited by Paul in 8:1. And yet the abuses at Corinth are such that, if they appeared in a modern congregation, the pastor would probably tear out his hair in desperation, or write the congregation off as a lost cause! These people who were so 'spiritual' had allowed parties to develop in the church, each faction claiming special allegiance to one of the missionaries who had worked at Corinth (1:12); they allowed a case of gross sexual immorality to go unchecked (5:1–5); they thought nothing of dragging each other off to heathen courts for justice (6:1–8); some had obviously not given up the sexual licence that stamped their old heathen existence (6:9–20); others were apparently doubtful whether a spiritual person could still have any sexual relations or should even marry (chapter 7). They abused their freedom by offending weak consciences in the matter of eating meat offered to idols (chapter 8), abused the *agape* (love-feast) and Lord's Supper (chapter 11), and even denied the physical resurrection (chapter 15). Little wonder that Paul called their spirituality into question and thought nothing of their 'knowledge'.

It is interesting to note that one of the key-verbs in the letter is *physioun* ('to puff up'). In 5:2 Paul calls his readers 'puffed up' (RSV has 'arrogant'). The verb appears earlier in 4:6,18,19 to describe the spiritual arrogance of these people. To their claim to knowledge, Paul retorts, '"Knowledge" puffs up, but love builds up' (8:1); and his description of Christian love as 'not jealous or boastful', literally 'puffed up' (13:4), is surely a cutting remark against the background of the Corinthians' lovelessness. It is as though Paul is saying: 'Yes, you are full of something, but whether it is the Spirit of God is another question. The Spirit is present among you. You have faith, and you have the Spirit's gifts, but you are also full of your own sinful human spirit. You are like a lot of toads puffing and blowing yourselves up into grand proportions with your own pride and vanity!' 1 Corinthians shows the apostle involved in a necessary piece of deflating. The readers' spiritual balloon had to be pricked to bring them back to the Gospel, to holiness, to love.

We may well ask how these Christians could allow such abuses and contradictions. How could they adopt a judgmental attitude against others while demanding for themselves absolute freedom to do as they liked? How could they have in the same congregation sexual licence and the renunciation of marriage and all sexual relations? As we ponder this problem, it is valuable to note that both these ideas—rigorous self-renunciation and full self-indulgence—were features of later, developed Gnosticism. And both features can be traced back to the false idea that man is divided into two separate parts—body and soul, or flesh and spirit. Obviously, if the spirit or soul is the higher principle in man, and if salvation means simply the redemption of a person's soul or spirit, the two contradictory ideas can arise. Either the flesh or body must be utterly suppressed to safeguard the purity of the spirit (hence self-renunciation), or the redeemed spirit is so above and separate from the body that the appetites of the body cannot affect it (hence self-indulgence).

Whatever their exact error, the Corinthians were certainly guilty of fleeing from material responsibility and from holiness in the body because of their understanding of spirituality. And so Paul had to remind them that their **bodies** were temples of the Holy Spirit (6:19). He also had to remind them that to have the Spirit did not mean release from the body at the end, but the resurrection of the body (chapter 15), since they had probably been smugly claiming that they had already experienced their spiritual resurrection by the power of the Spirit, like the heretics in 2 Tim. 2:18.

From our brief analysis of the problems at Corinth, it would seem beyond doubt that a loveless boasting in the possession of the Spirit and His gifts lay behind the abuses of these gifts. There seems to have existed a rivalry among the Corinthians in the exercise (and possession) of gifts, so that the women also were caught up by this enthusiasm to the point that all semblance of order in the congregation was being destroyed (11:2–16; 14:33–36; see the stress on order in 14:33,40). One may be forgiven for suggesting that the Corinthian theme-song seems to have been 'Anything you can do, I can do better'!

Paul had to teach the Corinthians in no uncertain terms that the Spirit gives His gifts for the harmonious growth and up-building of the whole church, not for private use or for personal aggrandizement. The possession of a gift can never be the basis for any boasting or pride at all. It is important to note a slight change in stress between Romans 8 and 1 Corinthians 12 and 14. In Romans 8 Paul speaks of the Spirit as the assurance of salvation, the power behind the believer's personal faith, love, and hope. In 1 Corinthians the emphasis is on the Spirit's role within the whole corporate church, the Body of Christ. These two emphases are not contradictory, but complementary. The Spirit is Christ's Spirit at work, perfecting the work of the Lord in the life of each believer. But the ultimate aim of the Spirit, as of God's entire plan of salvation, is the creation of a new people who will serve and glorify Him. The individual and corporate aspects are simply the two sides of the one coin. The two belong together: the personal experience of the Spirit in the life of faith, love, and hope; and the common experience of the Spirit within the fellowship of believers, the saved and serving people of God.

1 CORINTHIANS 12

Since a vast amount has been written on 1 Cor. 12–14 we shall restrict our comments to only the most necessary. The chief lessons of **chapter 12** are the following:

1. From the outset it is clear that Paul did not have to instruct his readers in the fact that there **are** spiritual gifts. They had written to him for instruction on the use of these gifts since there had been some controversy on this matter (7:1; 8:1 and 12:1 show Paul replying to a letter from the Corinthians themselves).
2. Paul immediately states that the work of the Spirit is Christ-oriented; His task is to produce faith and the confession to Christ; the heathen world may have its own spirits, but only the Holy Spirit can lead men to confess 'Jesus is Lord' (vv. 2,3). The stress is on Jesus, since the readers seemed to want only the glorified Christ and not Him who suffered on the cross. The Spirit still testifies to God's action in history despite all the humanity and weakness of that divine event!

3. It is important to note that the Corinthians had asked about *pneumatika* (spirit-gifts); and Paul uses this word when referring to the letter he had received from them (12:1; 14:1). But in giving his own teaching he prefers to speak consistently of *charismata* (grace-gifts). This change of terms (see 12:4,9,28–31) is surely not accidental. Paul knew that the Corinthians were proud of their possession of the Spirit and of gifts. He did not deny that there were special concrete gifts of the Spirit; what he wanted them to understand was that every special manifestation of divine *charis* (grace) in the form of a *charisma* is a pure gift. With all their rivalry and boasting they had forgotten that the Spirit's gifts were as much a matter of grace as the gift of the Spirit Himself.
4. Just as Christ cannot be divided (1:13), so also the Spirit and His gifts are a unity. Paul emphasizes the 'same Spirit' (12:4,8,9), 'one and the same Spirit' (v. 11), and 'one Spirit' (vv. 9,13), thereby reminding the Corinthians that the unity of the church is threatened not only where there is false allegiance to men (1:12), but also where various gifts of the Spirit are played off against each other.
5. The unity of the Spirit and His gifts corresponds to the unity of the Body of Christ. In fact, the unity of the body itself is traced back to the activity of the 'one Spirit' in Baptism (12:13). Incorporation into the Body of Christ is the first gracious activity of the Spirit. As **all** have experienced this gracious implanting, so **all** have received a gift. No one has been left out or overlooked.
6. All gifts are **given for service** to others, not for private gratification (not even for the personal assurance of salvation). They are given 'for the common good' (v. 7). It is presupposed that each man has his *charisma*, but in each case the gift means living for others, not for self. Thus, in 1 Cor. 7:7 Paul can call even one's vocation a grace-gift, an opportunity for service.
7. All gifts belong together within the unity of the body, for no member can exist independently of the rest of the body with all its other members. No gift has outstanding or absolute importance by itself; all the gifts are **mutually interdependent** for the life and health of the body. Some gifts may be more indispensable, just as some parts of the human body are more important than others (the blood-pumping heart is surely more vital than a toe-nail); however, there are no unimportant members, and no unimportant gifts, in the Body of Christ—only degrees of humble service.
8. There is some sequence or order in the list of gifts; there are 'higher gifts' (v. 31). Apostles, prophets, teachers, evangelists, pastors appear at the head of the list in Eph. 4:11 as well as 1 Cor. 12:28. This is surely so because these functions which require their own *charisma* deal with the Word by which the church is built and grows. But apart from this distinction there is no stress on *charismata* as special, supernatural manifestations of the Spirit. The Corinthians appear to have valued more highly the obviously-spectacular, supernatural gifts like tongues (as chapter 14 shows); Paul, while regarding all gifts as of supernatural origin (as gifts of God's Spirit), speaks of gifts of the Spirit which are anything but spectacular. The speaker in tongues or

the miracle-worker is **no more a charismatic** than the one who has the gift of generosity, mercy, administration, and the like (see also Rom. 12:6–8). Not the nature of the gift by itself, but its use and function within the total body is important.

9. No person can claim or demand a special **charisma** of his own choice. In 12:30 the idea that all can speak in tongues is not ruled out (see also 14:5); but that all do speak in tongues is clearly rejected. It is **not for man to choose** his own gift as if shopping in a supermarket with all the various *charismata* laid out on the shelves for each person to me his own choice! The Spirit 'apportions to each one individually as he wills' (v. 11). Heb. 2:4 says the same thing: 'gifts of the Spirit [are] distributed according to his own will'. One cannot dictate to the Spirit when it comes to gifts; where a gift is present it has been allotted according to the sovereign will of the Spirit.
10. 'This is the chief difference between the **fruit** of the Spirit and His **gifts**. Grace (*charis*) is the gift of the Spirit to **all** who are in Christ. To be a Christian without *charis* is a contradiction. The fruit of the Spirit arises as a gift of this grace to all men; faith, love, hope, joy, and peace are the 'natural' product of the Spirit's indwelling, for these are the blessings of Christ Himself to every Christian. A *charisma*, on the other hand, is a particular, concrete gift of *charis* which is given not to all, but individually as the Spirit wills (v. 11). This means that any Pentecostal demanding of a certain gift (e.g. tongues-speaking) as a sure sign of the Spirit is quite un-Pauline and completely unscriptural.
11. Paul's teaching on charismatic gifts makes clear a vital point which is often overlooked. Every Christian has experienced charis; but equally every Christian has some charisma. **Every Christian is, therefore**, according to Paul, **a charismatic** in the true sense of the word. This means that we today should not only 'earnestly desire the spiritual gifts' (14:1; 12:31); we should also alert each other to the gifts that the Spirit has already given us. How many gifts lie neglected and unused in the church, because eyes remain closed to the riches of the Spirit already there!

1 CORINTHIANS 13

The 'Hymn of Love', 1 Corinthians 13, obviously occupies a key position between chapters 12 and 14. The following necessary comments must be made.

1. In the argument against charismatics we sometimes find an incorrect use of 12:31b. It has been suggested that Paul tells his readers that they should seek love rather than spiritual gifts; this is quite impossible in the light of 12:31 a and 14:1,39. *Agape* (love) is not contrasted with gifts, nor is it advanced as a replacement for them. Such an argument misrepresents Paul, and has been quite rightly rejected by charismatics who argue the permanence of the spiritual gifts.

Paul begins his song of love with the statement: 'I will show you a still more excellent way'. Chapter 12 has already emphasized that the possession of a gift without its use for others is an abuse of that gift. Now Paul goes on to show how each gift should be used in love. The real contrast is not between gifts and love, but between a loveless claiming of gifts for oneself and a loving use of gifts for others.

2. The hymn of love is carefully formulated to come to grips with the abuses at Corinth. That lovelessness which the Corinthians had shown even at the Lord's Supper and the *agape*-feast (11:20–22) is further unmasked. Despite all their spiritual claims, their noisy tongue-speaking, prophetic power, and miracle-working faith had to be branded as futile and unspiritual without love (v. 13). And just because they had used their gifts to 'put down' fellow-Christians and to preen themselves in unspiritual, loveless pride, Paul penned v. 4–7 to put the positive contrasts of love in action.
3. The second half of the hymn of love prepares the way for Paul's discussion on tongues in chapter 14. Here he points to the temporary nature of both prophecy and tongues; both will pass away once 'the perfect' has come. It is best to take this reference to perfection as a pointer to the perfection of the Christian after the resurrection (chapter 15). Thus Paul does not say in this passage (v. 8) that tongues are limited only to the apostolic age or the Early Church. While this conclusion has been drawn from the passage, it is reading too much into the text.

Nevertheless, Paul does place a limit on tongues and prophecy, just as he points to the temporary nature of faith and hope in contrast to the permanence of love. There will come a time when the object of both faith and hope will be seen, and they will become obsolete. At that point, in eternity, we will see face to face the Lord whom we have believed in and looked for in hope. We will possess full and true *gnosis* (knowledge), not the supposed knowledge that the Corinthians were boasting about.

In what sense is tongue-speaking limited? The Greek term for speaking in tongues is *glossolalia* or *glossais lalein*. The verb *lalein* (to speak) is the same verb that Paul uses in v. 11 when he says: 'When I was a child, I **spoke** like a child, I thought like a child, I reasoned like a child; when I became a man, I gave up childish ways'. Paul is, of course, using the example of bodily growth as an example of growth from spiritual infancy to maturity. But the use of this verb is very revealing; it allows us to see Paul's true view of tongues. To Paul tongue-speaking is the lisping of a Christian in his infancy period. It is child's talk! This shows the absolute fallacy of the Pentecostal argument which asserts that tongues is the final proof of the Spirit, the sign of Christian maturity. In fact, the situation is the reverse. **Tongues belong to Christian infancy, not to maturity in Christ.**

1 CORINTHIANS 14

Once this is seen, Paul's statements about tongues in chapter 14 will be read correctly.

1. By misreading the accents of Paul, one can, indeed, find a strong argument for the permanence of tongue-speaking. Charismatics sometimes stress two verses out of context: 'I want you all to speak in tongues' (v. 5b) and 'I thank God that I speak in tongues more than

you all' (v. 18). However, in both cases Paul follows with a 'but'. Rather than pushing or enforcing the use of tongues, Paul points to a higher and greater gift, that of prophecy. Thus, in v. 5 he continues, "I want you . . . even more to prophesy', and in v. 19 adds, 'nevertheless, in church I would rather speak five words with my mind, in order to instruct others, than ten thousand words in a tongue'. How Paul can be made into the great 'apostle of tongues' after these statements is beyond comprehension!

2. Paul's argument again directs attention away from the possessor of a gift to the church as a whole. The key-words in the whole chapter are 'edify' and 'edification' (*oikodomein, oikodomē*). The final test of the validity, as well as the value, of a gift is the extent to which it edifies, or builds up, the church (14:3–5,12,18,26). Edification has nothing to do with an internal spiritual experience or 'emotional tickle'; it has to do with the up-building, strengthening, nurturing of the whole Body of Christ, within the fellowship of faith in the local congregation. Earlier in the letter, Paul had shown his special concern for the *oikodomē* of the church. '"Knowledge" puffs up, but love builds up' (8:1); '"All things are lawful", but not all things build up' (10:23b). Again we see how Paul remains singularly unimpressed by the mere possession of a charismatic gift.
3. Because Paul brings the discussion of tongues back to its proper setting—not private experience, but service within the church—prophecy must take precedence over tongues. The higher gift of prophecy is not one supernatural ecstatic gift alongside others; it is the **supreme** gift, since it is the conscious proclamation of God's work and will in Jesus Christ. That prophecy has nothing to do with religious ecstasy is made quite clear in v. 19; prophecy is speaking with one's mind. We could simply call it preaching. That there were prophets who predicted the future under the power of the Spirit has been seen from Acts 11:27,28 and 21:8–11; however, there is no suggestion that Paul is speaking of this prophetic activity here.
4. Why is prophecy greater than tongue-speaking? Speaking in tongues is private soul-talk with God, which, indeed, may give private edification, whereas prophecy gives a message to the whole church (vv. 2–5). The only way tongue-speaking can edify others is through an interpreter (v. 5). A tongue by itself is an unintelligible sound and indistinct note (vv. 7–9), and of no value for others unless it is deciphered. Paul goes so far as to say that one should keep quiet in the church if there is no one to interpret (v. 28).
5. Whereas tongues may or may not appear in the worship-service of the church, prophecy as the proclamation of the Gospel is indispensable to the gathering together of Christians. On the basis of Isa. 28:11,12, Paul argues that 'tongues are a sign not for believers but for unbelievers, while prophecy is not for unbelievers but for believers' (v. 22). But even this needs to be qualified. Uncontrolled tongue-speaking can easily be a confused babble of voices and turn the outsider away from Christianity, whereas prophesying or proclaiming

the truth in Christ will confront him with the Gospel even where there are a lot of people talking together (note the threefold emphasis of 'all' in v. 24).

6. Paul is finally concerned with order in the worshipping congregation. In 1 Cor. 11–14 Paul is actually ordering the worship-life of the church. The Lord's Supper and the proclamation of the Word belong at the heart of Christian 'coming together' (11:20); tongues do not. Indeed, they are more likely to be a disruptive influence in worship, which should be a common and corporate experience. God is a God of order (14:33,40), and the Spirit and His gifts belong to the order of God.

How much of the Corinthian aberrations were due to self-induced enthusiasm and ecstasy must remain an unanswerable question. The fact remains, however, that enthusiasm and ecstasy are by themselves no absolute proof that it is the **Holy Spirit** who is at work. The final impression left by the entire section on spiritual gifts is that Paul plays down the very thing the Corinthians boasted of—the spectacular, the obviously supernatural.

We need not draw exact parallels between the abuses at Corinth and much that is typical of Pentecostal teaching and practice; exact agreement does not exist. Neo-Pentecostals are also generally aware of the limitations that Paul places on tongues in 1 Cor. 14. And yet the over-evaluation of tongues in the charismatic movement reminds us of much that Paul had to fight against in 1 and 2 Corinthians. It is, indeed, ironical that just that Letter which is used to argue the importance of tongues, is Paul's greatest statement against an enthusiasm which has run off the rails and is in danger of losing the Gospel itself. The apostle would today be equally opposed to any enthusiast theology of glory. Here also the Word was written for our warning and admonition (1 Cor. 10:11).

Chapter VII

THE SPIRIT IN THE CHURCH TODAY

The Spirit is alive and well. He has not died, nor gone on holiday; He is as present in the church today as He was in the New Testament age. The continued existence of the church, despite frequent predictions of its death, is evidence enough of the continuing power of God's Spirit.

Our study has rejected the charismatic interpretation of many New Testament passages. In the process, we have stressed the point that the New Testament is truly charismatic in that the Christian's whole life of faith is a gift of *charis*, and his whole life of service involves the right use of the Spirit's *charismata*.

Our final task is to examine more closely the way in which the Christian experiences the Spirit today, and thus to give a positive scriptural answer to the sub-title of this book. This answer is directed to both charismatics and non-charismatics who claim to have experienced some special spiritual experience, and even some special charismatic gift. The answer is consciously Lutheran because the writer has the conviction that this is scriptural. The comments are rather directly related to the Lutheran Church, for that is the author's spiritual home and the arena of his primary ministry.

1. The Fundamental Experience of Grace

There are many Christians of sincere faith and genuine piety who have never had a heart-warming spiritual experience, have never had an overwhelming emotional sense of the presence of God. Some are not troubled by this, and would never desire such an experience; others, under pressure from charismatics, feel somehow to be deprived, second-class believers. The tragedy is that the desire for something extra can lead to a complete loss of the Gospel. The success stories of charismatics usually ignore the casualties, those who have not been able to feel the Spirit and have lost all faith whatsoever. Few books record these casualties, but many a pastor has met them when making his rounds.

To those who feel deprived and left out, and also to those who have had some experience, we say the following: To believe is to have the Spirit. **To be a baptized Christian and not have the Spirit is a contradiction in terms.** If you can make your sincere confession to Christ as your Lord, He and His Spirit are yours. To have Christ and not to have the Spirit of Christ is impossible.

Jesus and the Spirit are inseparable (Rom. 8:9,10; Acts 16:6,7 and John 14:16–18 show how Jesus and the Spirit are one). If, therefore, Christ lives in us by faith (Gal. 2:20), the Spirit also dwells in us. If there is still any doubt that we have the **fullness of the Spirit**, we should listen again to the words of the apostle:

'In him [Christ] all the **fulness** of God was pleased to dwell' (Col. 1:19).

> 'In him the whole **fulness** of deity dwells bodily, and you have come to **fulness** of life in him . . .' (Col. 2:9,10).

Because the believer has Christ, Paul can also give the Gospel command:

> 'Be **filled** with the Spirit' (Eph. 5:18), since his readers have been '**filled** with all the fulness of God' (Eph. 3:19)!

Because Christ had the Spirit 'without measure' (John 3:34), the believer does also.

Lutherans speak of the Word and the Sacraments as the Means of Grace, as the place where the Spirit is fully at work and where the Spirit is fully distributed. There is a very strong statement in the Lutheran Confessions which reads as follows:

> 'We should and must constantly maintain that God will not deal with us except through His external Word and Sacrament. Whatever is attributed to the Spirit apart from such Word and Sacrament is of the devil' (Smalcald Articles, III/VIII,10).

This statement, of course, reflects Luther's struggle against the Enthusiasts of his day (*Schwärmer*) who despised the external Word in favour of the 'inner light' or direct revelation through the Spirit. Religious Enthusiasm (from the Greek *en* and *theos*) is the cult of the god-within. But God offers His grace to us through the preaching of the Cross, no matter how humble. He offers His Spirit with all His regenerating and renewing power through the announcement of forgiveness in Absolution.

That is the graciousness of the Spirit. He remains over and above man, as much as He also dwells within him. The divine and the human are never united in the sense that man becomes divine. Nor can the Spirit be manipulated by human moral exertions or piety. Holiness itself is the work of the Spirit. He comes to those who are of humble spirit, who acknowledge that they are nothing but 'flesh' without Him. He comes in those humble Means of Grace which are so often despised as weak and ineffectual. He comes as grace, as gift, and all that men can do is to receive like beggars!

If we speak of the Sacraments as the home of the Spirit, we are not adding a new medium for the Spirit, for both Baptism and the Lord's Supper are the Gospel in action, or acted Gospel. In an anti-Gnostic statement, John points to Jesus who came in the flesh as the Son of God among men:

> 'This is he who came by water and blood, Jesus Christ, not with the water only but with the water and the blood. And the Spirit is the witness, because the Spirit is the truth. There are three witnesses, the Spirit, the water, and the blood; and these three agree.' (1 John 5:6–8).

Even if the prime reference in this rather cryptic passage is to the Christ, the incarnate Son of God, attested as such at His baptism and crucifixion, there are strong sacramental overtones.

The Spirit still comes in water and witnesses to the Son, perfecting His work 'by the washing of water **with the word**' (Eph. 5:26). One would wish that Lutherans (and others) understood the grace of Baptism better, for then there would be less uncertainty about the fullness of the Spirit. It is not accidental that charismatics very often show little understanding for the Sacrament as a water-and-Spirit Baptism (John 3:5; Titus 3:5). Where the one Lord, one faith, and **one Baptism** (Eph. 4:5) is no longer central to the Christian experience of grace, Where Baptism is no longer seen as the blessed act where God 'now saves' (1 Peter 3:21), there the Sacrament must be degraded into a mere sign or symbol.

Every baptism is a celebration of incorporation, again not merely a private experience. It is the Spirit's work not only to give faith in this sacred washing; it is also His work to plant the believer firmly into the Body of Christ, the fellowship of the Spirit. The communal, corporate work of the Spirit in the Sacraments comes out more clearly, however, in the Eucharist where the Spirit feeds the Body of Christ (the church) with the Lord's sacramental body and blood. Jesus Himself reminds us in His great discourse on the bread of life, and the flesh that He will give men to eat, that 'it is the Spirit that gives life' (John 6:63). Paul draws a close parallel between Israel's eating and drinking of 'spiritual' food and drink in the wilderness, and the eating and drinking by Christians in the Lord›s Supper (1 Cor. 10:3,4). The Corinthians who claim the Spirit, are in danger of abusing His gifts, also in the Sacrament, by their presumptuous attitude to grace. Paul's answer is: Do not despise God's spiritual gifts in the Sacrament!

The Lord's body and blood are present in the Sacrament simply because of the Lord's promise in the Words of Institution. However, because this is a meal in which Christ is proclaimed, we also know that it is the avenue of the Spirit's gracious work. Not the presence of Christ but the blessings of Christ are His special gift in this sacred meal.

A return to sacramental celebration is part of the answer to much of the subjective piety and theology of experience in the churches today. It is not by chance that Paul's words on the Lord's Supper immediately precede his teaching on spiritual gifts (1 Cor. 11 and 12). The Eucharist is the very heart of Christian life and worship. It is the three-dimensional fountain of faith: the re-presentation of Christ's death and resurrection as past events with present saving power, the celebration of His presence in and among the believing community now, and the proclamation of His future coming. (See how these three dimensions, past, present and future, are contained in Paul's words in 1 Cor. 11:23–26; the cry 'Our Lord, come!' in 16:22 is also a eucharistic cry, as the liturgical features of 16:19–24 indicate.)

When we speak of celebration we mean just that. It is just here that there is a great need in the Lutheran Church for a change of attitude and action. Changes are on the way, but for too long the celebration of the Sacrament has been marked by a one-sided emphasis on repentance and sadness, a kind of gloomy piety. The call for proper preparation has too often forgotten Luther's words that repentance **and faith are** the only marks of worthiness. In addition, communing has been seen as a private matter; we commune when we 'feel the need', when we have done the proper amount of soul-searching, perhaps when we have reached the right pitch of piety! It is still, not understood that the service with Holy Communion is the normal service of the Church, that the Eucharist is not an occasional appendix for the few. It is sad to hear the opinion that regular participation will lead to an abusing of the Sacrament, a despising of its special gifts; one could just as well argue that we should not read the Bible too frequently or hear too many sermons.

Where are we to find life and salvation in a more tangible form than in this meal? Where is there a greater, higher, more powerful, common experience of the Spirit than there where we kneel together to receive the Lord Himself? Where the Eucharist is no longer understood as a victory-celebration, as a meal of heavenly joy in which we are one with the saints of time and eternity ('Therefore with angels and archangels . . .'), it is completely understandable that some people will begin to look elsewhere for spiritual experience.

In addition to this appeal for a clear understanding of the Word and the Sacraments as the home of the Spirit, we need to make one more comment on the Word as the preached message of forgiveness. Great ages of spiritual renewal in the history of the church have usually been started by great preachers. The church today needs, as much as ever in its history, great Gospel-preaching. We will readily grant the point often made by charismatics that there is not enough instruction from the pulpit on the life of holiness and sanctification. But the fruit of the Spirit, faith, joy, peace, love, and hope, is produced not by ethical exhortation, but by the Gospel itself.

The Lutheran Church has always prided itself (sometimes with an all-too-human pride) on its preaching of the pure Gospel; the trouble is that much of the preaching is pure doctrine and nothing more. The New Testament word for preaching (*kēryssein*) suggests the action of a herald who has good news to proclaim in a bad situation. It is a joyful message of release, of freedom, of peace. But too often the sermon comes out as a tirade against all the evils of the world and the sinfulness of man, or simply as a collection of theological cliches in the process of reformulating a Bible story. If the preacher cannot reflect the joy of the Gospel in the pulpit, he can hardly expect his hearers to experience that joy in the pew. If he cannot show how the Gospel reaches into every minute corner of day-to-day existence, he should not blame his people for leaving their faith in the church after their one-hour stint of religion on Sunday morning.

The experience of the Spirit begins at the font; it is continued at the altar; it is continually fed from the pulpit and by family and private reading of God's Word. But all along the way it is a common experience of grace. It does not rest on subjective feelings or emotions, but feeds on the objective message of the Gospel itself.

To say, then, that the church does not possess the Spirit would be blasphemy; it would amount to a denial of grace. A pastor standing up in front of his congregation can never be sure who are believers and who are not. But he knows that there are always believers where God's Word is preached and where the Sacraments are celebrated, for the Spirit and His power are always there where these are present.

The real question for the Christian is not: Do I have the Spirit? but: Am I continually filled with the Spirit? (Eph. 5:18). If our devotion and spiritual life are weak, if our joy and peace fade, if the Gospel has lost some of its tang, that is not the fault of God and His Spirit. It is rather the fault of us sinful people who would prefer to hang on to something of the old ego and service to it, than to submit totally to the Lord who has bought us for Himself. The Spirit gives Himself fully, without reservations, without waiting for us to meet certain conditions. It is we who do not allow the Spirit to lead and direct us as He wants to.

If a Christian wants to remain filled with the Spirit (and not simply have an isolated momentary experience, however heartwarming that may be) the answer is quite simple. He does not have to go through a whole series of spiritual exercises; he does not have to 'tarry' or wrestle for the Spirit. He simply asks (Luke 11:13); he prays in the Spirit which he already has, sure that he will be built up in his faith (Jude 20). He clings to God's word of promise that he is a son of God; he reminds himself of his baptism where the Spirit first came to him. And he asks that Spirit to 'take over' his life and lead him from one day to the next in a life that is one long, unbroken 'spiritual worship' (Rom. 12:1). Above all, he allows the Spirit to come to him within the worshipping people of God, where he can with all God's saints praise the Spirit for the one experience of grace that never ends.

2. Evaluating Charismatic Experience

Where does this leave the charismatic who knows the Gospel, believes that he received the Spirit in Baptism and continues to do so in the Lord's Supper, and yet also knows that he has had a spiritual experience that has meant a new starting-point for his Christian life? What do we say to a person who agrees with most, if not all, that we have said so far, who rejects the Pentecostal doctrine of subsequence and consequence, but who has had an experience, perhaps also with speaking-in-tongues, which has transformed his life?

Lutherans, because of their cultural and ethnic background (in Australia most are of North European origin), seem to have a decided mistrust of a show of emotion in Christian piety; a 'Hallelujah!' or 'Praise the Lord!' in a Bible-study group is probably enough to cause considerable embarrassment for many! If one can venture a generalization, the American Blacks or Southern Europeans, for example, are far more volatile and free in the display of emotions than the more reserved, if not staid, people of Northern Europe.

Is the charismatic experience simply a matter of religious emotionalism conditioned by one's own character and ethnic background? While charismatics often appear to be people who are of a more emotional psychological disposition, it is also true that very unemotional characters have experienced charismatic phenomena. Emotionalism is not the whole answer.

Sociological and psychological studies in the past have tended to suggest that charismatic revivalism occurs especially with maladjusted individuals who are emotionally unstable or intellectually deprived. Glossolalia, or speaking in tongues, was traced back to such things as schizophrenia, hysteria, anxiety reaction, and susceptibility to auto- or hetero-suggestion. However, a recent study by Lutherans in the United States has not supported this view. One report of tests carried out on a limited sampling of 39 individuals did suggest that maturity affects the way in which glossalalia is used; the younger and emotionally-disturbed use tongues in a more 'bizarre' manner, while the mature employ it far more carefully. In addition, the studies suggested that charismatics tended to be very dependent on authority-figures, showing the same general psychological trait that is elsewhere called 'hypnotizability' (for a summary and evaluation of these reports see *The Charismatic Movement and Lutheran Theology, A Report of the Commission on Theology and Church Relations of the Lutheran Church—Missouri Synod*, January 1972, pp. 6–8).

While religious experience is open to psychological analysis (psychologists can, indeed, have a field-day at some revivalist meetings where emotionalism runs riot!), the charismatic will argue that his experience is not self-induced, but brought about by the Spirit of God, not by the spirit of man. The only other alternative is to see in charismatic phenomena signs of demonic power! It is certainly so that the devil will be just around the comer if we are close to God; indeed, the closer we are to spiritual things, the more we can be sure that the demonic will be present. Ask any honest pastor about the power of the Tempter, and he will have to admit that it is in the exercise of his holy duties, especially in preaching from the pulpit, that he is most fiercely attacked, especially with the temptation to pride.

The fact is that every faith has its own 'experience' which may or may not be explainable in psychological terms. Indeed, even if it could be shown that all charismatic experiences are psychologically conditioned, that would be no argument against their reality for those who have gone through an experience. God has in the past worked His wonders in ways that are also open to explanation in purely naturalistic terms; he can use earthquakes, tidal waves, and the like. Why should the presence of the Spirit not be marked by psychic phenomena without their immediately being branded as psychological abnormalities?

No, the problem is not that of religious experience or emotion itself. One might, indeed, wish that there were a bit more show of religious fervour and zeal, of love, peace, and joy, in many a congregation where religious piety demands a solemn, almost mournful, expression, sombre music, and a liturgical dignity that dare not be profaned by cracking a smile (no jokes in church, please, especially not from the pulpit!). The writer himself concedes that charismatic experience involves heightened emotions, a bubbling over of the human spirit which produces both peace and joy.

The real problem is how this experience is evaluated and interpreted within the whole Christian life. We are all different psychologically, and we have all had our 'religious experiences'. The writer can be moved to tears listening to a simple chorale or a more intricate Toccata and Fugue composed by that magnificent musician theologian, Johann Sebastian Bach; another person will be left cold. The writer can glory in Romans 8 as the (in his opinion) most magnificent statement of the Gospel in the whole of the New Testament; another Christian will experience his joy in the reading of another favourite passage. And while it remains true that taste can be educated to appreciate higher standards of perfection, there are those who experience greater joy in lustily singing Gospel-songs rather than chanting the liturgy or singing the ancient chorale tunes in the hymn-book.

To charismatics we consequently say the following: We accept the reality for you of your experience. But, from the outset, do not expect everyone to have the same experience as you have had, no matter how sure you are that it has been produced not by your own human spirit and its desires, but by the Holy Spirit.

The Lutheran confesses that he has been converted in his baptism, whether as an infant or as an adult (the latter makes no difference for we baptize adults as though they are infants, and infants as though they are adults, to quote one of the Church Fathers). Baptism is the beginning, not the end, of the Christian life. And, at any point in subsequent years, the whole truth of the Gospel can flood into one's person with new force and transforming power. The writer is of the conviction that many Lutheran charismatics with whom he has spoken have indeed had a new experience of the Gospel itself. In this sense we may speak of a new 'baptism of the Spirit'. But caution is strongly advised in the use of this term, since it has gained associations in Pentecostalism which are thoroughly unbiblical.

To say it again: Charismatics should not slight the grace and power of the Spirit in their past baptism and conversion by speaking of a new reception of the Spirit, which denies the fact that they have had Him all the time. They should humbly thank God for any experience, but leave their subjective experience and go back to the objective Word. In particular, we humbly offer the following pastoral advice:

1. Beware of making your experience the foundation of your faith. If you fail to make God's sure promises in the Scriptures the centre of your faith, you will have nothing to cling to, once the experience is gone! Be as suspicious of your own feelings and emotions as you are confident of the

truth of the Gospel as a message that did not originate with you, but came to you from God (1 Cor. 14:36).

2. Make sure that you do not succumb to the temptation to use your experience as a source of pride. Beware of the 'ego trip' which comes from an exalted evaluation of self because of some experience or spiritual gift. Above all, never boast of your experience or gift, or let others feel that they have missed out on the Spirit, that they are second-class Christians.
3. Make sure that your zeal for the Lord and your 'enthusiasm' in the Spirit, when questioned, do not lead you to enjoy a persecution-complex. The sects thrive on a persecution-complex. The more they are rejected as raving idiots, the more they are convinced they have the truth! Psychological studies have shown that ridicule, non-acceptance, and rejection often result in growth in charismatic circles. Where there has been no opposition, growth has been more difficult.
4. Beware of forming little closed groups within your congregation which breed suspicion and rumour because no one knows what is going on. Do nothing behind your pastor's back; he is your shepherd, and has the right and duty to supervise your spiritual life. If you have groups for Bible-study and prayer, let them be open, and be prepared to accept spiritual guidance.
5. Do not read your experience back into the Scriptures, for there is no fixed pattern of experience or piety in the New Testament. Do not make your style of piety a norm and standard that all must follow.
6. Finally, be prepared to give a good account of your faith in terms of the clear teaching of Scripture; an appeal to a feeling or an emotional experience will not do. The Gospel is not to be experienced with one's emotions alone, but, above all, with the intellect.

This last point is so important that it requires further explanation. The Christian faith is not only trust and confidence; it is also knowledge. It involves doctrine, a clear presentation of teaching, of faith-facts. One sometimes gains the impression that for charismatics, doctrine and clear theological distinctions are irrelevant; the important thing is to experience the Spirit.

If this position is really maintained, it must be met squarely. We must ask: Why did the New Testament writers waste so much time arguing about theological distinctions if they are unimportant? Why did Paul spend so much time defining justification? Was he only amusing himself or indulging in academic pride? Theology, and the making of clear confessions which embrace the whole truth of the Gospel, is not—or should not be—the concern of a few doctors in the church (they are, of course, placed in a position of special responsibility) but of the whole people of God.

Christian faith is, indeed, **experience through knowledge**. Consider the beautiful prayer in the Letter to the Ephesians, where Paul prays:

> 'That according to the riches of his glory he may grant you to be strengthened with might through his Spirit in the inner man, and that Christ may dwell in your hearts through faith; that you, being rooted and grounded in love, may have **power to comprehend** with all the saints what is the breadth and length and height and depth, and to **know** the love of Christ which surpasses **knowledge**, that you may be filled with all the fulness of God.' (Eph. 3:16–19).

The believer has both Christ and His Spirit dwelling in him. But this is not just a feeling; it is knowledge. That knowledge is, of course, more than a collection of facts; it is experiential knowledge, but it remains a recognition and comprehension of facts which can and must be confessed if others are to know the truth. The Christian does not witness to the God-within, but the God-without, that is, as He is found in Scripture and in the Sacraments. If we speak only of 'what Jesus means to me' (as important as it is that our witness be that of those who themselves know the truth), anyone has the right to answer: 'But that is what you have experienced. That's how you see it!' The saving truth existed long before we experienced or knew about it (1 Cor. 14:36).

St. Paul relegates tongue-speaking to a minor role simply because it does not sound a clear and intelligible message. Still today, the world above all needs a good account of the faith and hope that we have (1 Peter 3:15), not with an appeal to an experience that defies description, but in a carefully formulated and reasoned argument. The Christian faith may at times defy the understanding of the human intellect; it is beyond reason, but that does not make it irrational.

Christian knowledge comes not from introspection, from listening to a quiet little voice within, not from looking at the stars, not even from prayer (the latter is our speaking to God, not His speaking to us). It comes from preaching (Rom. 10:14–17); it comes from teaching, instruction, and learning of God's Word (1 Tim. 4:11–16; 2 Tim. 3:14–17). When Paul prays for his congregations, his standard prayer is for knowledge (Eph. 1:16,17; Phil. 1:9; Col. 1:9,10).

This brings us to a final point of concern. Charismatics generally love to search the Scripture. But the way in which the Bible is read often gives cause for concern. We are not referring to the hunting up of biblical precedents for experience to which we have referred above, but to the tendency to treat the Bible as a kind of storehouse of the Spirit with immediate relevance for today without any relation to the original meaning of the text or the historical situation in which it was spoken. The writer has attended a group Bible-study where the Bible was treated like a spiritual Pandora's box which could be opened and immediately used to reflect the reader's own thoughts, experiences, hopes, and feelings, without any effort at discovering what the text was really saying.

We are not suggesting that the message of the Gospel is not clear in Scripture, nor that its message is not relevant for today. The point is that its exact message must first be determined by close attention to context, logical progression of thought, and simple grammar. A special 'spiritual' reading of the Bible, which ignores the actual, original meaning of words and sentences, does not do glory to the Spirit who first gave us the Bible!

There is, of course, the truth that a certain passage of Scripture may 'come alive' for me at a certain point. It may have added meaning **for me** far beyond its original scope and intention. But the meaning of a text **for me** does not determine its meaning as it was written in the first place. Correct reading of the Bible begins with a prayerful attitude and with spiritual thirsting, but it is carried through by placing oneself **under**, not **over**, the Word.

Again it should be said that the dangers noted in this charismatic use of Scripture are not limited to neo-Pentecostals; they have no mortgage on reading things into the text!

3. The Charismatic Gifts Today

We shall presently look at the charismatic 'specialities' of tongues, prophecy, and healing; our immediate concern is to look at the whole range of gifts mentioned in the New Testament, and to face the basic questions of their meaning and permanence within the church.

There is no standard listing of *charismata* in the New Testament, nor can there be a standard number in the church today. The lists that we have are the following:

Romans 12:6–8: prophecy, serving, teaching, exhortation, liberal giving, giving aid, showing mercy.

1 Cor. 1:5–7: all (kinds of) speech, all (kinds of) knowledge.

1 Cor. 7:7: vocation, marriage, continence or virginity (see vv. 8–31).

1 Cor. 12:4–11: speaking wisdom, speaking knowledge, faith, healings, working miracles, prophecy, distinguishing between spirits, tongues, and interpretation of tongues.

1 Cor. 12:28–31: apostles, prophets, teachers, workers of miracles, healers, helpers, administrators, tongues, interpreters.

Eph. 4:11,12: apostles, prophets, evangelists, pastors, and teachers.

1 Peter 4:10: preaching, service.

Actually, the New Testament nowhere calls these gifts 'gifts of the Spirit'. More correctly, they are gifts of God given to the church through His Spirit, or the gifts of Christ Himself (1 Cor. 7:7; Eph. 4:7).

In addition to these lists, we have an occasional use of *charisma* without any reference to a specific spiritual gift. In Rom. 1:11,12 Paul looks forward to his arrival in Rome, and hopes that he will be able to share 'some spiritual gift [*charisma*] to strengthen you, that is, that we may be mutually encouraged by each other's faith'. The exact nature of the gift cannot be predetermined; God would simply provide some gift as Paul and the Roman Christians communicated the Gospel to each other. That any gift is a grace-gift is made clear also in Rom. 5:15–17: death came through one man, Adam, but the **free gift** of life (*charisma*) has come with **grace** (*charis*) found in the New Adam, Jesus Christ. Charismatic gifts are manifestations of the Christ-life in us! Eternal life is itself the great free gift (*charisma*) of God in Christ (Rom. 6:23).

The connection between grace and grace-gift is so close that Paul can use the word *charis* itself for the gift of his own apostolic commission (Rom. 1:5; 1 Cor. 3:10). The word 'grace' by itself, thus, sometimes refers to Paul's special gift of the apostolic office (see also Rom. 12:3; 15:15; Gal. 2:9; Eph. 3:2,7,8; and Phil. 1:7). In the Pastoral Letters, on the other hand, *charisma* is used for the gift of the pastoral office which was conferred on Timothy with the laying on of hands and the prayer (and gift) of the Holy Spirit (1 Tim. 4:14; 2 Tim. 1:6,7).

Are all these gifts for ministry of equal importance? One thing surely stands out in all the lists (apart from 1 Cor. 7). There is some kind of order in the gifts insofar as those gifts which mean service and ministry in the Word, in the communication of the Gospel, are placed first. Intelligible speaking comes before ecstatic speaking; the preaching ministry comes before the serving ministry (*diakonia*).

A 'hierarchy' of gifts is also suggested by Paul's words in 1 Cor. 12:28, 'first . . . second . . . third . . .' In addition, we have seen that 1 Cor. 14 clearly teaches the superiority of prophecy over tongues. Charismatics generally argue against any order of priority and importance in these lists, especially those in 1 Corinthians, since Paul says in 12:24 that in the body of Christ greater honour is given to the inferior member. However, this argument is quite unconvincing, since 12:24–26 does not refer to the importance of gifts, but to the honour and value of every single member in the church. There are no dishonourable members in the body of Christ. All have some gift, no matter how humble. The armpit and the toe-nail may not be very prominent in the body, but they still serve the whole body. There may be lowly functions in the church, but all are important.

One other distinction must be made. At the head of the lists in 1 Cor. 12:28 and Eph. 4:11 come apostles and prophets. Eph. 2:20 speaks of them as the foundation of the church, Christ being the chief cornerstone. We have earlier remarked on the unique character of the apostolic office. With the death of the last apostle, the office died out. But this office was unique in another sense. As has often been pointed out, the apostles and prophets were ministers to the whole church. They did not exercise their ministry merely within the local congregation (as true as it is that the local congregation is fully church). Peter was an apostle to the circumcised, whereas Paul's commission was to the Gentiles or uncircumcised. It is likewise clear that the prophets had a 'roving commission', as we might call it. That this special universal office died out rather early in the church is a fact of history, though there is no indication within the New Testament itself that this would be, or had to be, the case. The church manual called the *Teaching of the Twelve Apostles* or *Didache*, which dates from the end of the first century in Syria, reflects the fact that prophecy had fallen into some disrepute since false prophets and 'free-loaders' had been abroad in the church (chs. 11–13).

The fact that the apostolic office was a limited office, and that the universal prophet also disappeared from the scene in the Early Church, raises a question against the charismatics' claim that **all** gifts mentioned in the New Testament are meant for **all** time. While there is no clear evidence in the New Testament that these gifts would all disappear in time (they obviously have not all disappeared), there is no evidence that they **must** always **be present** in the church through all ages.

The problem with the charismatic position is that it stresses the obviously-supernatural and ecstatic gifts to the detriment of the others which are more mundane. It uses tongues and miraculous healing as proofs of the Spirit in a way that is foreign to the New Testament.

Remarkable in the lists are those gifts which highlight the use of the fruit of the Spirit which is love. Both Rom. 12:6–8 and 1 Peter 4:10,11 list works of love, mercy, kindness, and generosity. Putting a large cheque in the offering-plate in church, or giving generously to a needy cause out of Christian love, is as much a charismatic gift as speaking in tongues (2 Cor. 8 and 9). The Spirit means first and foremost **loving** service (1 Cor. 13).

Remarkable also is Paul's teaching on **vocation** as a *charisma* in 1 Cor. 7; the contents of the whole chapter show that a Christian's calling (*klesis* and *kalein* are the key-words in 7:17–24) or station in life, whether married or unmarried, whether slave or free, is a God-given opportunity of grace to live a life of service to one's fellow-man and to the glory of God. Indeed, it is just here that we detect one of the great dangers of charismatic thinking. In the laudable desire to serve God and witness to the Gospel with power, the call to service in one's daily life and vocation is overlooked. There reappears the old danger of making a distinction between one's religious and secular life, as though God is served 'properly' only when one is worshipping and witnessing. Luther's doctrine of vocation is sadly missing in the church's preaching and teaching today. Christians need to rediscover the witness of life in vocation before grasping eagerly at the witness of the Word. One can also roast a dinner, hammer in a nail, operate a computer, or drive a tractor to the glory of God! These do not replace Christian witness to the Gospel itself, but that witness in word can never be a replacement for a life which is seen as ministry in its totality. The person who is so intent on witnessing, even on speaking in tongues and prophesying, that he at the same time neglects his practical duties, does God no honour. The mother who neglects her family chores, no matter how menial, in the pursuit of higher and more noble 'spiritual ministry', the father who does slipshod work at his trade in order to escape away to 'real' spiritual work for the Lord, is side-stepping his first God-given duty, his prime *charisma*. We can presuppose that Paul remained an efficient tent-maker all his life—as well as faithful apostle!

We do not know exactly what all the gifts in the New Testament lists mean. Attempts have been made to define the exact function of these gifts, but the task is futile and never results in final conclusions. We do not know, for example, what Paul means precisely by 'helpers' in 1 Cor. 12:28. And it is certainly not so that the 'pastor' mentioned in Eph. 4:11 can be identified with the pastoral office in the church today. The very fact that Paul does not give us anything like a standard list reflects his basic concern: to point to the **many ways** in which the Spirit equips the whole church for ministry. Our task is not only to seek, desire, and pray for gifts, but to alert each other to the gifts that we already have, and to encourage each other in a loving use of each gift so that others will be served in love.

There is one final observation which places a great question-mark against the preoccupation (if not obsession) with supernatural gifts. It is a fact which seems to have escaped most people's attention, but one which is surely significant: St. Paul mentions the obviously supernatural gifts only in his First Letter to the Corinthians. None of the other lists mentions miracles, tongues, interpretation of tongues, and healing. From this it cannot be concluded that Paul speaks of these gifts with tongue in cheek, as if he were questioning the reality of these gifts in the Corinthian congregation. But he is writing to people who certainly have an over-exalted opinion both of themselves as Spirit-people, and of certain spectacular gifts which they possess. That Paul lists these gifts last is, therefore, highly significant.

If we grant that these special gifts can occur at any time and place in the church, we will also be eager to see that they are properly evaluated, and that every claim to a special gift is carefully tested.

4. Prophecy

We turn now to a brief discussion of those charismatic gifts which are claimed by neo-Pentecostals as special signs of the power of the Spirit in the church today, and which are often linked with a 'baptism of the Spirit' as the second experience of grace. We again look not at what is claimed to be prophecy today, but at the New Testament itself for the truth of the matter; the danger of reading present practices back into the New Testament must be warned against once more.

Charismatics agree that prophecy is different from speaking in tongues since it involves a clear and intelligible presentation of God's will to edify, encourage, comfort, and teach the hearer. It can convict the unbeliever, for it is first and foremost the clear declaration of human sin and divine grace.

However, they claim that prophecy, like glossolalia, comes as a direct, immediate revelation of the Spirit, and is uttered in an ecstatic or semi-ecstatic state. It does not arise from any conscious intellectual activity on the part of the speaker, but reveals truths directly given by the Spirit. Sometimes the interpretation of tongues is also called prophecy. This view, based on 1 Cor. 14:5, seems to arise out of an attempt to salvage tongues from a position of lesser importance compared with prophecy. Tongues, we are told, are indeed a lesser gift by themselves, but tongues plus interpretation are on the same level of importance as prophecy.

Pentecostals have held that such revelation through direct prophecy is equally authoritative with the revelation of God in Scripture. Neo-Pentecostals, to the best of our knowledge, reject this view: they affirm the Reformation principle of *sola scriptura* (Scripture alone is the authoritative revelation of God and His will), and stress the need to test every prophetic utterance carefully according to Scripture (1 Cor. 14:29; 1 John 4:1). Nevertheless, they have a high regard for prophecy. While tongues are not for all, the gift of prophecy should be earnestly desired by all (1 Cor. 14:1–3,5,39). While the prophetic gift does not lead to new truth over and above Scripture, it leads to a new and vital understanding of Scripture itself, to inspired preaching, teaching, and application of the Word. While prediction of the future may occur, this is not the chief feature of prophecy.

A brief look at the New Testament shows that the nature of prophecy in the Early Church is not always immediately clear. Certainly there were people with the title 'prophet' who functioned alongside the apostles in the whole church. Apostles and prophets are mentioned together in Eph. 2:20; 3:5; 4:11; 1 Cor. 12:28. This office was a gift not given to all (1 Cor. 12:29). Acts 11:28 and 21:8–11 refer to Agabus who was a prophet not only in Jerusalem, but also in Antioch and Caesarea: whether the four daughters of Philip mentioned in the second passage had a permanent, prophetic gift is not clear. The activity of these prophets certainly included the revealing of the future, and the choosing, by revelation from the Spirit, of men for spiritual office (Acts 13:1,2; 1 Tim. 1:18; 4:14). But it is likely that their chief task was to expound the Scriptures of the Old Testament under the guidance of the Spirit, the same Spirit who had first moved the Old Testament prophets themselves (1 Peter 1:10–12). Their duty was to explain the mystery of God's will and plan (1 Cor. 13:2; Eph. 3:3–5; Rom. 16:25). In this sense, Paul at times seems to regard himself as a prophet, although his apostleship was his prime calling (see especially Eph. 3:3–5).

On the other hand, Paul encourages every Christian to seek the *charisma* of prophecy (1 Cor. 14:1), without thereby implying that all must become 'prophets'. He infers that every Christian can prophesy; there is no limiting of this gift as with others (12:29,30). The characteristics of this kind of speaking are understanding God's mysteries (13:2), upbuilding, encouragement and comfort, instruction and learning (14:3,19,31). That exhortation was a chief function of the prophet becomes clear in Acts 15:32 where we read of two prophets, Judas and Silas, who 'exhorted the brethren with many words and strengthened them'.

There are two books in the New Testament which prominently show both the features of prophecy—the interpretation of Scripture, and its direct application to the readers. The first of these is Hebrews. The unknown writer of the Letter to the Hebrews calls his writing a 'letter of exhortation' (Heb. 13:22). He uses the same phrase or term employed to describe an exhortatory address in the Jewish synagogue made on the basis of the Old Testament (see Acts 13:15 where Paul is invited to give the 'address' in the synagogue at Antioch in Pisidia). Hebrews actually gives us a long sermon expounding a series of Old Testament texts as they apply to Christ and then bringing to the readers comfort and encouragement in view of the persecution and pressure they had suffered (Heb. 10:32–34; 12:1–11). Thus Hebrews is a series of exhortations interposed with scriptural expositions, all meant to ground the readers in a firm faith so that they will not waver from the truth or flinch under suffering.

While the book of Hebrews does not expressly call itself prophecy, Revelation clearly does so (Rev. 1:3,10; 22:19). This book again illustrates the nature of prophecy as encouragement and comfort. It is also a message for the future which works with Old Testament references and allusions.

Prophecy thus means a direct expounding of God's will so that its meaning for the present and future is made clear. It exposes 'the secrets of his [man's] heart', but leads from a knowledge of sin to faith (see how closely 1 Cor. 14:24,25 is paralleled by Heb. 4:12,13). The teacher in New Testament times no doubt also expounded Scripture, and while the two gifts of teaching and prophecy are separated in Rom. 12:5,6, 1 Cor. 12:29, and Eph. 4:11, Paul presupposes that both gifts could be held by one person. But the prophetic gift meant more than exposition. It meant a direct application of the text by the power of the Spirit.

However, the New Testament gives us no cause to believe that prophecy must be ecstatic or semi-ecstatic speaking. John simply says that he was 'in the Spirit on the Lord's day' (Rev. 1:10), a phrase which may or may not denote an ecstatic state. Dreams and visions need not involve ecstasy. Paul speaks only of revelations coming to, and being made by, the person with a prophetic gift (1 Cor. 14:30); there is no further instruction on the mechanics of this speaking. What we do know is that the person with the prophetic gift is not turned into a mindless robot, without any self-awareness or self-control. In commanding order in the use of the gift, Paul says 'the spirits of prophets are subject to prophets' (14:32); the speaker knows and understands fully what he is saying, and can stop speaking at any moment. There are, of course, cases in the New Testament of involuntary prophets, men who are not exactly kindly disposed to Jesus and the disciples, and yet who prophesy the truth without realizing it; we think of Caiaphas in John 11:50,51, Pilate in 19:19–22, and perhaps Gamaliel in Acts 5:33–39!

We can readily understand why the prophetic gift and office were very much alive in the Early Church. The living voice of the apostles and prophets had to serve the church until it had the written Word of the New Testament canon. We have 'the prophetic word made more sure' (2 Peter 1:19) in the full apostolic witness of the New Testament.

Does this mean that prophecy is dead? The answer is most certainly No! If prophecy is the direct proclamation of Scripture so as to reach the heart (and not just the mind) of the hearer, if it means taking God's Word and applying it directly to every situation of human life, if it means encouragement, comfort, and assurance, one would hope that every preacher in every pulpit has the gift of prophecy. That this is not always the case will be obvious; not every sermon is scriptural, not every address means a real and vital confrontation with the truth so that one's faith is deepened, one's love fanned into a new flame, one's hope set alight once more. The *charisma* of prophecy is a gift that every pastor, preacher, and Christian teacher ought to pray for. To reach people's hearts with just the right word at the right moment, to speak to them and not **over** or **past** them, is a great spiritual gift. But the captive in the pew all too often gets words, words, and more words, with no Word from God; he gets high-sounding doctrinal dissertations, Bible stories, insipid moralizing, and easy solutions to problems which do not benefit the hearer.

There are biblical commentaries which are superb pieces of accurate scholarship with minute details relating to philology, grammar, historical background, context, and the like; they explain the words of the biblical text in great detail, but still do not communicate the Word. To proclaim the Word is a spiritual gift which cannot be learned in the class-room, not only because it is a gift of the Spirit, but also because it is exercised in love, the fruit of the Spirit. The communicating of the Gospel as prophecy means loving and understanding those who must hear the Word.

But what of private prophecy in a small group, for example, in a Bible-study session? We do not doubt that the Spirit can move any Christian to understand new depths and dimensions of Scripture, and to pass them on to others; truth is not the private domain of trained pastors and theologians. But here several points are important:

a) all such prophetic interpretation of Scripture must not ignore or destroy the primary and obvious meaning of the text (we still need scholars to help us understand that meaning);

b) all prophecy must be according to the analogy of faith (Rom. 12:6); any prophecy that conflicts with the truth revealed in Scripture is to be rejected as false and not of the Spirit;

c) any predicting of the future which does not rise out of the sure promise of God contained in the Gospel itself is to be treated, at best, with reserve. God's future will for us is clear enough in the New Testament itself; any seeking after detailed knowledge of future events arises not from faith but from un-faith.

5. Speaking in Tongues

When we turn to the activity of speaking in tongues (glossolalia), what a confusion of tongues we face! The books and articles which deal with the pros and cons of this question are legion; we have everything from emotional pleading for tongues to passionate rejection of such mumbo-jumbo, everything from exegetical studies on the New Testament evidence to personal testimonies, case studies, and psychological analyses. In all the babble of voices and opinions one is reminded of the story of the tower of Babel in Gen. 11:1–9 where man, trying to make a name for himself, tries to scale the celestial heights to reach God, and God comes down and scatters mankind into many nations each with its own tongue. There are those who seek to reverse the process and see in tongues the supernatural language by which divided mankind will again be able to talk a common united language with God; tongues—not the Gospel of oneness in Christ (Eph. 2:11–22)—will bring Babel in reverse, we are told!

Pentecostalism has itself been one of the most divisive influences in the church, not because of its claim that tongue-speaking is still a living gift of the Spirit today, but because of the way this gift is viewed and evaluated. The classical Pentecostal view is that glossolalia is the necessary sign of the second blessing, the special baptism of the Spirit after conversion. In addition, the special charismatic gift of tongues is to be valued highly since it is the special divine language of praise and gives personal assurance that one has the Spirit.

Our studies in Acts have already rejected this view of tongues. We repeat the basic findings which show the fallacy of the Pentecostal position:

1. The sign of tongues marked not a second experience of the Spirit, but a first, that of conversion itself.
2. Tongues are not a **necessary** sign of the Spirit's coming or filling. On three occasions the reception of the Spirit was accompanied with tongues—Jerusalem (Acts 2:4); Caesarea (10:44–46); Ephesus (19:6); on other occasions no such speaking was mentioned.
3. There is no set pattern of Christian experience in terms of a sequence of events, let alone a set biblical precedent. Neither Jesus nor the apostles promised or commanded tongues as a gift to all Christians in all ages. Pentecostals who use the baptism of Jesus as a precedent for a second 'baptism of the Spirit' are silent on the fact that Jesus Himself never spoke in tongues!
4. Where tongues are mentioned in Acts, we can understand in each case why a special sign was necessary. The Spirit marks crucial turning-points in the church's growth and mission by such special signs. The demand for tongues as a universal sign is legalism of the worst possible order.

It is therefore a relief to meet Lutheran charismatics for whom speaking in tongues is no longer a live issue, and who reject the standard Pentecostal errors. They even admit that tongues is 'child's talk'

(1 Cor. 13:11) and has only a limited function. However, it is still generally a characteristic of charismatics that they hanker after the gift of tongues as a special sign of the Spirit. And if one hankers hard and long enough, some special sign will come; whether it will be a genuine speaking of the Holy Spirit, or self-induced ecstasy with an overflowing of the human spirit, is another question!

In general, charismatics argue as follows: A distinction must be drawn between tongues as a sign of a special filling of the Spirit in Acts, and glossolalia as a special charismatic gift in 1 Corinthians. In the latter, tongue-speaking is a gift not given to all, but is to be valued by all. It may be a special supernatural tongue or a known language; there can be either tongues of men or of angels (1 Cor. 13:1). It is to be valued since it is the language of exalted praise to God (14:2), it is the soul-talk of the Spirit by which a believer is comforted or edified (Rom. 8:26,27; 1 Cor. 14:4), and the unbeliever is struck by the power of God's Spirit at work (14:22). Charismatics argue that Paul still lists tongues alongside prophecy (14:26) as profitable for the whole church. They meet the objection that tongue-speaking is a divisive factor in the church with the counter-argument that only the improper use of tongues and their absolute rejection by non-charismatics are divisive. They point out that Paul does not reject tongues, but unruly, undisciplined, proud, and self-centred use of tongues.

In our brief study let us look at four questions which come to grips with the chief problems: Are there different kinds of glossolalia? Do tongues exist today? What is the nature of glossolalia? What is its purpose and proper use?

1. **Are there different kinds of glossolalia?** The distinction made between tongues in Acts and 1 Corinthians is correct, for the same reasons stated above. In the one case, we have signs of the Spirit's presence in conversion itself; in the other, we have a special continuing gift. There is no evidence in Acts that those who spoke in tongues at their conversion continued to possess this gift afterwards, and the nature of their tongue-speaking seems to be different from that in 1 Corinthians. At Pentecost the diaspora Jews from around the eastern world clearly heard the apostles speaking their own native language (Acts 2:11). It can be argued that the tongues in 10:46 and 19:6 were also intelligible to the hearers. At least Peter and his six companions knew that Cornelius and his companions were praising God; in Acts 19, Luke reports that the Ephesian Christians 'spoke with tongues and prophesied', and the two terms linked here can be understood as two forms of intelligible speech—ecstatic and non-ecstatic.

Whatever the case may be in the last two instances in Acts, the tongues spoken of by Paul seem to be only unintelligible sounds, not languages known to mankind somewhere on the globe. 1 Cor. 14:10,11 may suggest that Paul thought of a tongue as an unknown language, but this is not the necessary conclusion; he may simply be using the analogy of an unknown language to illustrate the unintelligibility of tongue-speaking.

2. **Do genuine tongues exist today?** Paul concedes the use of tongues in Corinth to people who 'are eager for manifestations of the Spirit' (1 Cor. 14:12). He is obviously not interested in either establishing their use or wanting tongues to be given greater prominence; the opposite is the case. But the very existence of the gift **then** is enough to suggest that it is a gift that the church may experience **at any time**. We have argued that 1 Cor. 13:8,9 cannot be used to prove that tongues were temporary or that they were limited to the Early Church. As with prophecy as a special charismatic gift, we can understand why the Early Church perhaps saw a great deal of this gift, even more than is suggested by a few references in 1 Corinthians. Before the formulation and acceptance of a New Testament canon, such manifestations of the Spirit had special point.

It is another thing to suggest that every claim to tongues in our day is a claim to a genuine gift of glossolalia. We are repeatedly reminded of the fact that ecstatic speech is not confined to Christianity. John Sherrill in *They Speak with Other Tongues* (see the report on p. 84) records the fact that the Mormons in Nauvoo, Illinois, spoke in tongues in the middle of the last century—and Mormonism is certainly not Christianity! The well-known writer Kurt Koch makes the strong statement:

> 'Heathens, and Christians, possessed people and tribal dancers, witch-doctors and spiritists can all speak in tongues. The tongues movement is the expression of a deleterious condition through which a breaking in of demonic powers manifests itself (1 Tim. 4:1).'

He further makes the same observation as psychologists have made, that charismatics are very dependent on authority-figures. The laying on of hands, joining hands, etc. suggest dependence on a medium as in spiritistic circles (see *The Strife of Tongues*, p. 46f). Nevertheless, Koch also admits that there are genuine cases of speaking in tongues on record, despite the fact that almost all the case-histories examined in his brief study are seen as examples of pseudo-tongues.

Granted that ecstatic speaking is not limited to the church; granted that much of what passes for tongues is simply the result of reaching an emotional pitch through wild music, singing, and dancing, even rolling on the floor and such frenzied actions; and granted that there is also ecstatic speaking which shows the power of the demonic as in spiritism; there are still enough cases which strike one as genuine, precisely because of the lack of any special ecstatic state, to suggest that this charismatic gift still exists today.

As long as there is one case of glossolalia which conforms to the New Testament limits set by Paul, and can be interpreted as a confession to Jesus Christ as Lord and a praising of the mighty acts of God (1 Cor. 12:3; Acts 2:11), we must concede that this charismatic gift was not limited to the apostolic age—even if studies have shown that it soon fell into both misuse and disuse (see the brief but excellent history of tongue-speaking in A. A. Hoekema's *What About Tongue-Speaking?*, pp. 9–33).

3. **What is the nature of glossolalia?** Since it is not easy to identify genuine cases of tongue-speaking, it is easier to answer the question: What is the nature of ecstatic speech? A practising psychiatrist recently reported to an Australian Anglican Committee, set up to make an enquiry into neo-Pentecostalism, that speech similar to speaking in tongues has been observed

a) in a baby's babbling speech;
b) during a patient's freaking out on lysergic acid;
c) from a patient suffering from an overdose of amphetamine drugs;
d) as a severe side-effect of major tranquillisers;
e) in the repressed speech of the acute psychotic;
f) in sleep-talking.

(see *Both Sides to the Question. Official Enquiry into Neo Pentecostalism*, The Church of England Diocese of Sydney, 1973, p. 26).

Another expert suggests that 'glossolalic experience . . . is abnormal. It is a form of dissociation within the mentality of a person. It is in reality a separation which blocks off the rational function of the brain with the result that action is produced apart from rational control. Temporarily the speaker has entered a pathological condition . . .' (D. W. Burdick, *Tongues—To Speak or Not to Speak*, p. 84).

Studies in America at the Lutheran Medical Centre in Brooklyn came to the conclusion that while there were bizarre cases, the tongue-speaker did not suffer from some psychological abnormality. Speaking in tongues is not gibberish, but appears to have its own rhythm and linguistic quality, even if it does not have the normal characteristics of a human language (*The Charismatic Movement and Lutheran Theology*, p. 8). However, anyone hearing tongues for the first time, at least loud noises that are claimed to be tongues, will usually be struck with the dissonance of the noises produced: guttural groans, harsh whispers, shrill cries. In such cases one is justified in adopting a very sceptical attitude to the claim of tongues!

However, there does not appear to be any standard form of ecstatic speech. The most convincing cases that the author has experienced involved barely-audible whispers by persons who were anything but obviously-emotional ecstatics. And there are those charismatics who insist that there have been cases of tongues where an actual language, unknown to the speaker, was spoken, or where a tongue assumed the 'shape' of a real language with certain linguistic patterns and rhythms (see John Sherrill, *They Speak with Other Tongues*, pp. 110–113).

The fact that ecstatic speech involves some kind of psychological dislocation or switching off of the mind, does not prove that there can be no genuine glossolalia today as Spirit-motivated speech. The Spirit can use normal and abnormal psychic states alike. But the above comments only make more urgent our next question.

4. **What is the purpose and proper use of a tongue?** Quite apart from Paul's limited evaluation of tongues, it is clear that the New Testament as a whole places a great stress on Christian knowledge, on clear thinking, on surrendering one's whole life to the Spirit—not on the surrender of one's mind to irrational states.

The only positive thing Paul can say about speaking in tongues is that it is a speaking to God (presumably in prayerful praise), which may edify the speaker. Charismatics testify to the wonderful feeling of peace which ensues after speaking in a tongue.

As long as the Christian understands the limits of glossolalia, the practice should cause no consternation in a congregation as long as the following points are acknowledged:

a) Not every form of ecstatic speech must be glossolalia. For example, the murmuring of such words as 'Hallelujah' or 'Shalom', or snippets of Bible texts (usually from the Authorized Version!), are no evidence of supernatural tongues.

b) Tongues are a private matter, not for display in the worship service of the congregation, certainly not as a standard part of the Sunday liturgy.

c) There dare not be any coercion of others in order to convince them they must have this gift, nor any suggestion that they have missed out on a great gift.

d) The Christian who thinks he has a genuine gift will test that gift rigorously; rather, he will allow it to be tested by others. He will ask whether it is not simply a result of his own religious fervour and zeal, arising when an emotional pitch has been reached. Above all, he will allow the gift to be tested according to the rule of 1 Cor. 12:3: only the Spirit of God calls forth confession of Christ.

e) The speaker in a tongue should be aware that the suspension of normal mental activity leaves one open to the invasion of other less-than-holy spirits who will pervert praise of God and confession to Christ into self-glory, pride, and the denigrating of 'ordinary Christians'!

f) While not accepting any and every claim to tongue-speaking, the non-charismatic members of the congregation should not be shocked or affronted by the emergence of ecstatic speech; they should lovingly help any person with a genuine gift to use it properly and humbly to the glory of God.

g) There should be no despising of tongues but a genuine desire to accept any strange manifestation that is part of a spiritual experience, provided that it is tested. Even speaking that is the result of heightened religious zeal and emotions, and not a genuine tongue, need not be wrong or evil by itself.

h) **Christians should reject any attempt to use tongues as a proof of the Spirit, and trust only in the possession of the Spirit by faith, and, above all, in the promise of their baptism. They should resist any attempt to make tongues anything more than a peripheral feature of Christian experience.**

Without attempting to denigrate tongues as such (and thus disobeying the injunction of Paul not to forbid such speaking), one must say that the Pentecostal stress on tongues as central to Christian experience must finally lead to a very low opinion of the Spirit's work and power. For if tongues is the great sign of the Spirit today, one must come to the conclusion that the Spirit is rather impoverished. What our world needs is a clear voice, a clear witness, not unintelligible and confused sounds. An unbeliever who can hear the same sounds in a mental institution, a clinic for drug addicts, or a spiritist seance, will hardly be led to conviction of the Holy Spirit's power. He needs the Gospel, not tongues!

6. Divine Healing*

The heading of this section is deliberately so formulated. For the usual term 'faith-healing' reflects part of the confusion in this area. Faith does not heal, as little as faith justifies. We are justified by God's grace in Christ, **accepted** in faith; we can only experience divine healing as a gift of God asked for and **received** in faith.

The question at issue here is not whether God **can** heal, but whether He always **must** heal. Charismatics say that because Christ and the apostles healed, and because Paul speaks of the *charisma* of healing, and James 5:13–18 promises the effectiveness of prayer for healing, Christians should pray for divine healing without doubting that it is God's will that salvation includes wholeness of body and mind. The basic inference in all this is that all sickness and suffering is a sign of the devil's power. Involved in this question is the further suggestion that healing is integral to the total ministry of the church, and that a ministry of the Word without healing is, therefore, only a part-ministry.

Those who object to this charismatic argument should not too quickly assert that all supernatural healing has a naturalistic explanation, or that charismatic healings simply use hypnosis or the power of auto- or hetero-suggestion. We are told by authorities in the matter that physical diseases very often involve psychological causes. And there may be more than a trace of hypnotherapy in some 'faith healing', although this certainly does not apply in all cases. Moreover, Jesus is reported to have used some standard techniques with suggestive connotations when He healed; He put His fingers into deaf ears, and spat and touched bound tongues and closed eyes.

On the other hand, the statistical argument based on verified healings cannot be used to determine the rights and wrongs of divine healing. Fakirs and wonder-workers are cheaper by the thousand in human history!

* Much of this section is taken from a paper first delivered to the pastors of the Queensland District of the Lutheran Church of Australia in August, 1965, and later printed under the title 'Is There a Ministry of Healing as an Integral Part of the Ministry of the Church?', *in The Australasian Theological Review* Vol. XXXVII No. 4 (Oct.–Dec., 1966), 124–133.

Remarkable cures have occurred, but the problem is that these are not always evidence of the Holy Spirit's power. Quite apart from the many cases of sheer fraud and deceit, of fakery and quackery, the heathen world has its own healers with supernatural claims to power (the Australian tennis player, Tony Roche, has had his own success, according to reports, with a Filipino faith-healer). Spiritism, Christian Science, and other non-Christian groups claim healing powers.

The Roman emperor Vespasian is said to have possessed healing power after his acclamation by the troops. George Fox, the Quaker leader, Charles II of England, and the famous healing shrines of Roman Catholicism at Lourdes and elsewhere have all been associated with healing powers. The problem is not that our world will not accept miraculous cures, but that there are too many claims made to make them all credible. In any case, the student of the Bible knows that the demonic has its own signs. The false prophet of Deut. 13:1–5 could work miracles, just as the magicians of the Egyptian pharaoh could match their skills with Moses and Aaron (Exod. 7:11,22; 8:7)—at least up to a point (Exod. 8:18). Jesus warned His followers to look out for the false christs and prophets who would later appear producing their own signs and wonders and leading the elect astray (Mark 13:22). The Apostle Paul also predicted the coming of the 'lawless one' whom Satan would equip with a magnificent array of signs and wonders to deceive and hoodwink people (2 Thess. 2:9–11)! As long as we do not fully understand the psychosomatic nature of both sickness and healing, and as long as miraculous healing is not always an indication of divine power at work, any claim to Christian healing will not be substantiated by the mere claim that 'it works'. The real evidence of **Christian** healing will lie not in healing itself, but in the way it is related to faith in Christ and to the Gospel itself.

That a ministry of healing within the whole church is the chief issue can be seen from the 1964 Report to the General Convention of the American Episcopal Church, reprinted in the New Zealand publication *Wholeness* (No. 29, Feb. 1965). On page 5 we read the following:

> 'Throughout the book of Acts it is implied that the power to heal is an apostolic gift. . . . Every ministry and service of the Church is a healing ministry and service. This revival of the healing ministry of our Lord is bringing about a great spiritual renewal within the Church. . . . The Church's ministry of healing, then, is vital in our Lord's plan for the salvation of the human race. If as a member of the priesthood of all believers, every Christian is of necessity involved in the Church's ministry of healing, it is obviously true that every ordained clergyman is also involved. . . . There is, thus, no room for the permissive latitude of an 'either/or' arrangement in the matter of a ministry of healing. As a part of the priest's overall pastorate, the therapy of a healing ministry is not an optional one.'

The church has throughout its history experienced the healing hand of the Lord in answer to the promise of Ps. 50:15: 'Call upon me in the day of trouble; I will deliver you, and you shall glorify me'. But the above excerpt from the Report indicates that more is demanded than what is viewed as an occasional half-hearted appeal to God for help—after the doctor has been consulted! What is being promoted is a fully-organized approach to healing on the part of the whole church and its total ministry. In the face of this, the following points must be emphasized:

1. That our Lord's ministry was also a ministry of healing cannot be disputed. But His works of healing, reported in the Gospels, must be seen within the perspective of His total mission. We can take the account of the healing of the deaf-mute in Mark 7:32–37 as an illustration of the way in which Jesus' miracles are to be interpreted. After using sign-language to awaken trust and faith in this man, Jesus speaks the one word, 'Ephphatha', that is, 'Be opened'. The word is surely not directed to his tongue and ears as if they will answer His call (after all, the man is deaf!). What we have is a creative word which calls the whole man to be open to the call into the Kingdom. The stereotyped, choir-like response of the onlookers at the end of the story is not merely a piece of superfluous editorial interpretation on the part of the evangelist himself. It points to the central meaning of the miracle of healing. The crowd says: 'He has done all things well'. This is an echo of Gen. 1:31 where God the Creator, looking on His handiwork, passes His final judgment: 'And behold, it was very good'. In other words, the work of Jesus is the continuation of the work of the Father; it is the recreation of a fallen mankind, or a new creation (2 Cor. 5:17). Sin, suffering, and death are signs and symptoms of creation in its fallen state. The kingdom of God now bursts in on this world with its own signs which involve the destruction of sin, suffering, and death. There is another piece of theological reflection contained in the text. The crowd adds: 'He even makes the deaf hear and the dumb speak'. This statement sees the fulfilment of Isaiah's vision of a new creation which will be ushered in with the arrival of the Messiah. 'Behold, your God . . . will come and save you. Then the eyes of the blind shall be opened, and the ears of the deaf unstopped, then shall the lame man leap like a hart, and the tongue of the dumb sing for joy' (Isa. 35:4–6). With Jesus these last times have finally arrived. God is at work, beginning His new creation, the creation of a whole new humanity.

This one example shows how Jesus' healing ministry takes up Old Testament themes, and is one aspect of His total ministry of calling men back to God. Above all, Jesus is, according to Matt. 8:17, the Suffering Servant of God of Isa. 53:4 who 'took our infirmities and bore our diseases'. The ministry of the church begins with Christ the Servant, who came to serve, not to be served, who humbled Himself under the will of the Father even to His death on the cross (Mark 10:45; Phil. 2:8).

It should be noted that, to the eye of an onlooker, there was little difference between Jesus' miracles and the healings, exorcisms, and other miracles of others at that time. The Hellenistic world had its many wonder-workers in Jesus' day; healings were also claimed for rabbis and healers in the Roman world. Jesus' miracles can be understood only when seen as a part of His preaching of the Gospel of the Kingdom. They certainly serve to authorize Him as God's divine agent, but they also illustrate His ministry as a message of mercy.

2. That the power to heal was also an apostolic gift is also not open to debate. But the question again is: How does this gift fit into the total ministry of the apostles, and was it a gift that they handed on to the ministry of the church for all times?

We have spoken above of the role of the apostle as an authorized eye-witness agent of the risen Lord. As an ambassador or representative of the Lord, the apostle has full authority to act and speak on Christ's behalf, as if Christ were Himself acting and speaking. We thus naturally expect the apostles to continue the healing acts that were a part of Jesus' ministry. Already during the Lord's lifetime on earth, the disciples were sent out to preach and heal in His name. They were sent out with His power (*dynamis*) and authority (*exousia*) according to Luke 9:1,2. Paul, a late-comer on the scene, but no less an apostle through his confrontation with the risen Lord, joined the ranks of the other apostles who had the power to heal 'in the name' or 'through the name of Jesus Christ' (Acts 3:6; 4:30), and this even after the Lord's ascension. Three points should be noted in the healing accounts in Acts:

a) Luke is concerned to show the line of continuity between the Lord and His apostles (even if Paul is not called an apostle in the strict sense in Acts). Thus Peter says to Aeneas, 'Jesus Christ heals you' (Acts 9:34). And the continuation, 'Rise and make your bed', together with the reaction of the crowd, is surely meant to remind the reader of Jesus' own healing of a paralytic in Luke 5:17–26 (or Mark 9:1–8). This last miracle also has its apostolic counterpart in the healing of the lame man at the Gate Beautiful in Acts 3:1–10. And just as Jesus healed with the mere touching of the hem of His robe (Mark 6:56) so even Peter's shadow had healing power in Acts 5:15.

b) The apostolic ministry of healing (to retain this phrase) was only part of their total ministry, only an accompaniment to their preaching of Christ. We find no trace of a separate healing ministry. Healing is never a demonstration of supernatural power, never a performance, never an end in itself; it always arises from and serves the proclamation of the Gospel.

c) The New Testament church was fully aware that it was living in last times which had begun with the resurrection of Jesus and the outpouring of the Holy Spirit at Pentecost. They viewed the continuance of miracles of healing as a 'natural' sign that the rule of God had come and that He was continuing His creation of a new people. But nowhere is there any indication that signs and miracles must continue in the same way for all times, nor is there any indication that the apostles passed on gifts of healing to others.

Certainly Philip also worked exorcisms and signs (Acts 8:6,7); however, the American Episcopal Church's statement that healing was a special apostolic gift is not only correct—it must be specially stressed. The very unique character of the original apostolate implies that, just as not all features of Jesus' ministry were transferred to His apostles, so not all the powers of the apostles were handed on to the later church. The successors of the apostles, that is those who preach and teach the apostolic Word, have not been automatically granted the gift of healing.

3. Before we look at Paul's letters and the *charisma* of healing, we should also note what the New Testament means by healing. A study of the word-group for healing in the New Testament and the early Church Fathers shows that healing was never seen purely in physical terms. For example, Luke uses the verb *iaomai* ('heal') in both Luke 5:17 and Acts 9:34 in much the same way as the Greek Old Testament (the Septuagint) uses *iaomai* to translate the Hebrew verb *rapha*, a favourite word especially of the prophet Isaiah (see Isa. 6:10; 53:5; Job 5:18), which meant the healing that comes with the forgiveness of sins. Thus the New Testament sees healing as a temporal manifestation of the reception of salvation itself (also in German *Heilung* and *Heil* are related words). But by the time we reach the Apostolic Fathers, *The Shepherd of Hermas*, Barnabas, and 1 Clement use the verb 'to heal' (*iaomai*) only in the sense of healing of sins. They understood that this was the vital healing offered by Jesus and the apostles. While special gifts of healing may have still existed in post-apostolic times, there is not the slightest indication that the church felt itself called on to practise physical healing as an integral part of its ministry.

4. On the other hand, the New Testament knows of charismatic gifts of healing given to individuals quite apart from the apostles. The assertion that the whole church must be involved in healing, that the whole priesthood of believers should exercise this ministry is denied by Paul in 1 Cor. 12:9,28; it is a special *charisma* given as the Spirit wills. Quite clearly, not all receive the gift (vv. 11 and 30); Paul speaks not of the duty or obligation of all to heal, or even to pray for healing, but of special healing powers given to a few. The gift of healing did not belong to the essence of being a Christian, but remained an individual gift of grace. That Paul does not see the whole church as involved in healing should be perfectly clear.

   In a sense, Paul makes an office of this *charisma*; but he does not place the Spirit under an office, but makes the bearer of the Spirit with his special gift an office-bearer. Only in this individual sense can we speak of an office or ministry of healing in the New Testament.

5. Important to the charismatic argument for divine healing is **James 5:13–16**:

   > 'Is any one among you suffering? Let him pray. Is any cheerful? Let him sing praise. Is any among you sick? Let him call for the elders of the church, and let them pray over him, anointing him

> with oil in the name of the Lord; and the prayer of faith will save the sick man, and the Lord will raise him up; and if he has committed sins he will be forgiven. Therefore confess your sins to one another, and pray for one another, that you may be healed. The prayer of a righteous man has great power in its effects.'

Charismatics argue that this text proves the case for faith-healing which simply takes the promise of Scripture at face value. Where there is no healing, there is a lack of faith. Faith has its own power. In answer to this interpretation, which superficially seems correct, the following should be noted:

a) It is necessary to determine whether this passage contains a piece of general or specific exhortation. That is, does the command to anoint and pray over the sick apply to the office of the elder in the congregation, or does it reach beyond the circle of elders? Does the mention of elders refer to all leaders in the congregation or only to those who have special gifts of healing?

b) The oil used in anointing is hardly thought to have special healing powers when used by an elder; it is rather symbolical of the gift of the Holy Spirit Himself and His power to save the sick person. The laying on of hands is not even mentioned, nor is it a necessary rite for healing.

c) There does not seem to be any reason to believe that the office of elder makes the prayer for recovery any more effective. The command is: Pray for each other, that you may be healed (v. 16). The verses under scrutiny occur in a section which deals with the efficacy of prayer, not with the powers of an office. Thus we are not dealing with special charismatic powers of healing, but simply with prayer.

d) The real question is: **Must** the prayer of faith be answered? The charismatic will want to say Yes. However, the passage does not say as much, despite v. 15. If we took this verse literally there would be no such thing as sickness in the church, at least not for any length of time.

e) There is no new teaching on healing here in contrast to the Old Testament, where the believer knows that he can call on God for help in any trouble, including sickness. The prayers of righteous men have always found a merciful hearing with God. There is also no evidence of a special charismatic ministry in the church as a part of its total ministry.

f) In any case, we cannot be absolutely sure what James means by the verbs 'save' and 'raise' in v. 15. The most natural interpretation is not to take v. 15 as a promise of healing and complete restoration (unconditional at that), for the Greek words used (*sōzein* and *egeiren*) are the verbs used for the eternal saving of man and his being raised at the Last Day!

g) That v. 15 refers to his final salvation and not a temporal healing is also suggested by the emphasis on the prayer for forgiveness. If the sick person confesses his sins and accepts forgiveness, then the promise that he will be 'healed' in all eternity is, indeed, an absolute and unconditional promise, for it is the promise of the Gospel itself.

h) Thus it is most likely that only v. 16 refers to temporal healing from physical sickness. And here there is no promise that the man will be healed. We simply have the command: Pray that you may be healed. The prayer presupposes trust in God's power and mercy, but does not presume on God's grace!

Thus James 5:13–16 neither teaches that the church has a ministry of healing nor that God will always answer prayer with healing. It simply encourages Christians to pray for each other, and attaches a great promise to prayer.

6. The really important question in this whole issue of divine healing is the nature of prayer and the way in which God answers it, and, in particular, God's will with respect to healing itself.

While sickness and death are signs of man's sin, and indeed sickness can be the direct result of human sin and folly (think of the glutton and the alcoholic), the New Testament does not allow us to see a direct causal relationship between all sickness and sin. Nor can we say that all sickness is of the devil. There is also that hidden will of God which uses not only sickness, but even sin, for His plan!

The suggestion that God must always respond to our requests for healing with a show of divine power, reflects not great faith but a lack of faith in the providential care of the Father. To presume that we know always what is best for us is to take the place of God.

While there is that faith which dares to take the promise of the Lord seriously to pray in His name and expect an answer (Mark 11:24; John 16:23,24), neither the charismatic gift of healing nor our prayer give the sure prospect of healing. We have no right or power to place God and His Spirit under duress, or to force His hand. The prayer for divine healing which turns God into a tame little puppy-dog who must obediently follow our beck and call, which turns God (to change the image) into a jack who must pop out of his box when we press the right faith-button, does not arise from true faith.

Sickness, when it did appear in the Early Church, did not give rise to surprise or dismay among Christians, even when the sickness remained permanent. They believed in divine healing; they witnessed miraculous cures. But they saw the Spirit as the guarantee not of healing, but of eternal life (Eph. 1:14; 2 Cor. 1:22, 5:5). And so Paul, who himself healed others, was left with physical ailments (Gal. 4:13–15 and 6:11 may suggest that his ailment was a sight-deficiency); despite his fervent prayers, he was left with his thorn in the flesh (2 Cor. 12:7–9). When Timothy suffered from a sick stomach, Paul did not recommend that he go to a healer but prescribed a common-sense medical remedy, a little wine (1 Tim. 5:23). And in other cases where we read of sickness (Epaphroditus in Phil. 2:26,27; Trophimus in 2 Tim. 4:20), there is no hint of a miraculous cure.

Every prayer of the Christian will be prayed in the Spirit of the Lord who said, 'Not what I will, but what thou wilt' (Mark 14:36). The Early Christians looked on healing as the object of prayer in the surrender of self to God and His will. John writes that we should pray confidently believing that 'if we ask anything according to his will he hears us' (1 John 5:14,15). And Paul reminds us that we really do not know how to pray as we should. The Spirit has to pray for us, for He knows the will of God (Rom. 8:26,27).

The New Testament does not know a ministry of healing. It knows only the one ministry of reconciliation (2 Cor. 5:18), the ministry of the Word (Acts 6:4), the ministry of testifying to the Gospel of the grace of God (Acts 20:24), the ministry of righteousness (2 Cor. 3:9), and the ministry of evangelism (2 Tim. 4:5). Nowhere is there a mention of healing as an integral part of the ministry of the church.

The above point surely suggests that special 'healing services' will not be a normal practice in the church and its worship life. Every public service is a celebration of grace commonly believed and commonly received. But that there may be gatherings of Christians with special prayers for the sick is to be expected where Christians take the words of James 5:16 seriously!

We readily agree with those charismatics who suggest that Christians should show a greater trust in the power of the Spirit to heal, that they should be more open to the special *charisma* of healing; but where charismatic insistence on healing rears its head, where faith becomes a quantity instead of a quality and is used to try to force God's hand, there we object loudly. For who knows how much damage to faith has been done by faith-healers who demand greater, deeper, stronger faith on the part of the sick person, and finally put the gift of faith itself in doubt?

It is all grace—the Gospel, the Spirit, faith, Baptism, gifts for ministry. And the Christian who cannot rejoice in the Spirit while he sings the song of grace, has not yet learned what it means to be led by the Spirit!

A SELECT BIBLIOGRAPHY

From the sea of literature on Pentecostalism and the charismatic movement we list a few titles for further reading.

A. Official Reports

The Charismatic Movement and Lutheran Theology. A Report of the Commission on Theology and Church Relations of the Lutheran Church—Missouri Synod, 1972.

Both Sides of the Question. Official Enquiry into Neo-Pentecostalism of the Church of England, Diocese of Sydney, 1973.
(These two official church reports attempt to give an unbiased assessment of the charismatic movement and its theology.)

B. Historical and General Studies

Hollenweger, Walter J. *The Pentecostals: The Charismatic Movement in the Churches* (Augsburg, 1972).

Bloch-Hoell, N. *The Pentecostal Movement: Its Origins, Development and Distinctive Character* (Allen and Unwin, 1964).
(Hollenweger's book is still the most detailed and thoroughly researched study. It is a critical but objective study—with a full bibliography—from one who understands the movement as an ex-Pentecostal minister.)

Brumback, C. *Suddenly . . . From Heaven. A History of the Assemblies of God* (Gospel Publishing House, 1961).

Kendrick, K. *The Promise Fulfilled: A History of the Modem Pentecostal Movement* (Gospel Publishing House, 1961).

Nichol, John Thomas. *The Pentecostals* (Logos International, 1970).
(Of these three histories written by men within the movement, that by Nichol is probably the best.)

Jorstad, Erling. *Bold in the Spirit. Lutheran Charismatic Renewal in America Today* (Augsburg, 1974).
(An attempt at an objective understanding of the movement allowing the charismatics to tell their own story.)

Kerr, John Steven. *The Fire Flares Anew. A Look at the New Pentecostalism* (Fortress, 1974).
(Contains helpful material on the early history of the church as well as social and theological aspects of the present-day movement.)

Jones, James W. *Filled with New Wine: The Charismatic Renewal of the Church* (Harper and Row, 1973).
(A critical but sympathetic review of charismatic claims.)

O'Connor, Edward D. *The Pentecostal Movement in the Catholic Church* (Ave Maria Press, 1971).

Ranaghan, Kevin and Dorothy. *Catholic Pentecostals* (Paulist Press, 1969).

(The best two studies on the charismatic movement within the Roman Catholic Church.)

Knox, R. A. Enthusiasm. *A Chapter in the History of Religion* (OUP, 1950).

Schaeffer, Francis. *The New Super-Spirituality* (Hodder and Stoughton, 1973).

(These two books, though not dealing directly with charismatics, are particularly helpful in understanding the place of the movement within the history of religious enthusiasm.)

C. Scholarly Exegetical Studies

Bruner, Frederick D. *A Theology of the Holy Spirit. The New Testament and Pentecostal Experience* (Hodder and Stoughton, 1970).

Dunn, James D. G. *Baptism in the Holy Spirit* (SCM, 1970).

Dunn, James D. G. *Jesus and the Spirit. A Study of the Religious and Charismatic Experience of Jesus and the First Christians . . .* (SCM, 1975).
(Solid reading, but still necessary for the serious student of the New Testament. Bruner's work is still the best available on the subject.)

Bittlinger, Arnold. *Gifts and Graces. A Commentary on 1 Corinthians 12–14* (Hodder and Stoughton, 1967).
(A good, popular treatment of these key chapters.)

Lampe, G. W. H. *The Seal of the Spirit* (SPCK, 1967).

Schlink, E. *The Doctrine of Baptism* (Concordia, 1972).
(These books are listed as helpful guides to an understanding of the work of the Spirit in the Sacrament of Baptism. Schlink's solid study presents the Lutheran confessional position.)

D. Critical Interpretations

Agrimson, J. Elmo, ed. *Gifts of the Spirit and the Body of Christ: Perspectives on the Charismatic Movement* (Augsburg, 1974).
(Six helpful essays from specialists in various areas examine the charismatic movement from various angles: theological, historical, psychological, and sociological.)

Barnett, P. and P. Jensen. *The Quest for Power. Neo-Pentecostals and the New Testament* (ANZEA, 1973).
(A critical analysis, including many sound biblical interpretations, by two Australian Anglican theologians.)

Burdick, D. W. *Tongues: To Speak or Not to Speak* (Moody, 1970).

Dillow, Joseph. *Speaking in Tongues* (Zondervan, 1974).

Duncan, George B. *The Person and Work of the Holy Spirit* (Lakeland, 1973).
(A simple, evangelical theology of the Spirit, with some balanced comments on the experience of the Spirit.)

Goodman, Felicitas D. *Speaking in Tongues. A Cross-Cultural Study of Glossolalia* (University of Chicago Press, 1972).
(A technical and scientific study of the phenomena of tongues.)

Hillis, D. W. *Tongues, Healing and You* (Baker, 1969).

Hoekema, Anthony A. *Holy Spirit Baptism* (Eerdmans, 1972).

Hoekema, Anthony A. *What About Tongue Speaking?* (Eerdmans, 1966).
(Hoekema's widely read critical studies offer much sound historical and biblical argumentation.)

Jorstad, Erling, ed. *The Holy Spirit in Today's Church. A Handbook of the New Pentecostalism* (Abingdon, 1973).
(A collection of essays with historical studies and an analysis of the present movement from writers on both sides of the question.)

Kelsey, Morton T. *Healing and Christianity in Ancient Thought and Modern Times* (Harper and Row, 1973).

Kelsey, Morton T. *Tongue Speaking* (Doubleday, 1964).

Kildahl, John P. *The Psychology of Speaking in Tongues* (Harper and Row, 1972).
(An attempt at an objective psychological analysis of the phenomena without final theological solutions to the problem.)

Koch, Kurt. *The Strife of Tongues* (Kregel, 1971).
(This well-known booklet, written by an authority on the occult and the demonic, comes to negative conclusions on the basis of case studies.)

Samarin, William J. *Tongues of Men and Angels: The Religious Language of Pentecostalism* (Macmillan, 1972).

Stagg, F., E. G. Hinson and W. E. Oates. *Glossolalia* (Abingdon, 1967).

Stolee, H. J. *Speaking in Tongues* (Augsburg, 1973).
(An older study, reprinted, which aims at a balanced and irenic discussion on this disputed topic.)

Stott, John R. W. *The Baptism and the Fullness of the Holy Spirit* (IVF, 1964).
(An excellent brief analysis of the biblical material relevant to the discussion of this central issue.)

Taylor, John V. *The Go-Between God. The Holy Spirit and the Christian Mission* (SCM, 1972).
(This award-winning book includes a section—chapter 10—on the charismatic movement. Solid, but rewarding, reading.)

Unger, Merrill F. *New Testament Teaching on Tongues* (Kregel, 1971).

Unger, Merrill F. *The Baptizing Work of the Holy Spirit* (Scripture Press, 1953).

Watson, David. *One in the Spirit* (Hodder and Stoughton, 1973).
(A small but helpful evangelical study written in a simple, but personally direct, style.)

Wietzke, Walter and Jack Rustad, eds. *Toward a Mutual Understanding of Neo-Pentecostalism* (Augsburg, 1973).
(A collection of articles presenting both sides of the question and attempting to keep the lines of communication open.)

E. Other Charismatic Literature

Baker, J. *Baptized in One Spirit* (Foundation Trust, 1967).

Bennett, Dennis J. *Nine O'Clock in the Morning* (Logos International, 1970).

Bennett, Dennis J. and Rita. *The Holy Spirit and You. A Study Guide to the Spirit-Filled Life* (Logos International, 1971).
(Two influential books by American Episcopalian charismatics.)

Christenson, Larry. *Speaking in Tongues. A Gift for the Body of Christ* (Fountain Trust, 1963).

Christenson, Larry. *Speaking in Tongues and Its Significance for the Church* (Bethany Fellowship, 1968).
(One of the first and certainly the most famous among Lutheran pastors to attempt an explanation of his charismatic experience.)

Frost, Robert. *Set My Spirit Free* (Logos International, 1973).
(A typical example of the work of this popular American charismatic.)

Harper, M. *Power for the Body of Christ* (Fountain Trust, 1964).

Harper, M. *As at the Beginning* (Hodder and Stoughton, 1971).

Jensen, Richard A. *Touched by the Spirit—One Man's Struggle to Understand His Experience of the Holy Spirit* (Augsburg, 1974).
(Recommended as a study by a Lutheran charismatic with some sound critical comments against much of the false theology current in charismatic circles.)

Kuhlman, Kathryn. *God Can Do It Again* (Prentice Hall, 1969).

Kuhlman, Kathryn. *I Believe in Miracles* (Pyramid, 1968).
(Two books from one of the most famous healers of our time.)

Lensch, R. *A Missouri Synod Lutheran Pastor Is Baptized in the Holy Spirit* (Wilkins, 1969).

Prange, Erwin. *The Gift is Already Yours* (Logos International, 1973).
(Two autobiographical books by American Lutheran pastors. That by Prange is helpful for Lutheran charismatics.)

Schepp, J .A. *Spirit Baptism and Tongues Speaking according to Scripture* (Fountain Trust, 1970).

Sherrill, John L. *They Speak with Other Tongues* (Hodder and Stoughton, 1967).

Williams, J. R. *The Era of the Spirit* (Logos International, 1971).

ADDITIONAL BIBLIOGRAPHY (COMPILED BY JOHN T. PLESS, 2019)

The preceding bibliography is helpful in providing exegetical resources written prior to 1976. It is supplemented by the following resources that focus on doctrinal, historical, and missiological works.

Bayer, Oswald. "God's Presence: The Holy Spirit." Pages 239–54 in *Martin Luther's Theology: A Contemporary Interpretation*. Translated by Thomas Trapp. Grand Rapids: Eerdmans, 2008.

Oswald Bayer, one of the most significant Lutheran theologians and Luther scholars of our day, notes that the Holy Spirit is "no apparition" (243) but true God, one with the Father and the Son. The section on the "External Word and Modern Spiritualism" (249–53) is particularly insightful as Bayer demonstrates that Luther does not search for the Spirit in the subjectivity of the self but in the objectivity of God's promise delivered by the Spirit in Scripture, sermon, and Sacraments.

Bruner, Fredrick Dale, and William Hodern. *The Holy Spirit-Shy Member of the Trinity*. Minneapolis: Augsburg, 1984.
Bruner (who is also the author of an earlier exegetical study, *A Theology of the Holy Spirit: The New Testament and Pentecostal Experience*) contributes chapters on the Holy Spirit and preaching and Baptism. Hodern's chapters treat the Holy Spirit in connection with the theology of the cross.

Commission on Theology and Church Relations. *The Lutheran Church and the Charismatic Movement*. St. Louis: The Lutheran Church—Missouri Synod, 1977.
Theological assessment of the Charismatic Movement from the perspective of confessional Lutheran theology.

Jenkins, Philip. *The Next Christendom: The Coming of Global Christianity*. Oxford: Oxford University Press, 2011.
In what one reviewer rightly called a "landmark book," Jenkins narrates the changes occurring as Christianity grows in the Global South even as it declines in Europe and North America. Significant sections of this insightful work are devoted to the exploration of Pentecostal phenomenon in world Christianity, especially in relation to syncretism.

Kärkkäinen, Veli-Matti, editor. *The Holy Spirit and Salvation: The Sources of Christian Theology*. Louisville: Westminster/John Knox, 2010.
This anthology contains primary sources of writings on the Holy Spirit from apostolic fathers to contextual interpretations of the present in Africa, Asia, and Latin America. This is a helpful and fairly representative source book.

———. *Pneumatology: The Holy Spirit in Ecumenical, International, and Contextual Perspective*. Grand Rapids: Baker Academic Press, 2002.
Written by a Finnish Pentecostal scholar, this book provides an overview of a historical-theological interpretation of the doctrine of the Holy Spirit. Particularly helpful is the descriptive presentation of the doctrine of the Spirit in contemporary theologians (especially J. Moltmann, C. Pinock, M. Welker, W. Pannenberg, K. Rahner, J. Zizioulas, etc.) and the treatment of various "contextual pneumatologies."

Lindberg, Carter. *The Third Reformation? Charismatic Movements and the Lutheran Tradition*. Macon, Georgia: Mercer University Press, 1983.
This is a valuable historical account that begins with Luther's struggle against the "Spiritualists" in the sixteenth century and traces a trajectory through Pietism as a "second Reformation" and then to the Charismatic Movement of the twentieth century as a "third Reformation." Lindberg does a fine job of laying out Luther's concerns regarding the Enthusiasts who divorced the

Word and Spirit. His treatment of contemporary charismatic phenomenon in light of Reformation theology is measured but deeply insightful.

Lockwood, Gregory J. *Concordia Commentary on 1 Corinthians*. St. Louis: Concordia, 2000.
Excellent discussion of speaking in tongues and prophecy in 1 Corinthians as well as a fine excursus on "Spiritual Gifts in 1 Corinthians" (426–54) by an Australian Lutheran New Testament scholar.

Ngien, Dennis. *Luther's Theology of the Cross: Christ in Luther's Sermons on John*. Eugene: Cascade Books, 2018.
Chapter 10, "The Glory of the Holy Spirit's Office: Economic Actions" (188–207), engages Luther's exposition of John 14–16. Ngien notes: "The Holy Spirit does not enlighten us with an unearthly glory; he establishes faith in Christ, contrary to reason and all appearances. Faith, a gift of the Spirit, is justifying faith, whose object is the crucified Christ" (197).

Opsahl, Paul D., editor. *The Holy Spirit in the Life of the Church*. Minneapolis: Augsburg, 1978.
This is a collection of essays assembled by the Lutheran Council in the USA (LCUSA) when the Charismatic Movement was at its height in Lutheran churches in North America. The essays reflect biblical studies and historical studies, reflections from systematic theologians, and pastoral concerns. The papers were originally given at regional conferences for pastors of the church bodies (ALC, LCA, and LCMS) that formed LCUSA.

Peters, Albrecht. *Commentary on Luther's Catechism: Creed*. Translated by Thomas Trapp. St. Louis: Concordia, 2011.
Detailed treatment of Luther's exposition of the Third Article of the Creed (209–306). Demonstrates that Luther understands the work of the Spirit in relation to Christ. The Spirit brings us to Christ and Christ to us in the Gospel. To use Luther's language, "the Spirit is like a poor lute-player who knows how to play but one song" (256).

Prenter, Regin. *Spiritus Creator: Luther's Concept of the Holy Spirit*. Translated by John M. Jensen. Philadelphia: Muhlenberg Press, 1953.
This is an older but important study of Luther's theology of the Holy Spirit by a prominent Danish theologian of the last century. The author deals with the "early" Luther's understanding of the Spirit in light of medieval theology in the first part of the book. The second part of the book is devoted to Luther's opposition to the Enthusiasts.

Sánchez, Leopoldo A. *Sculptor Spirit*. Downers Grove: IVP Academic Press, 2019.
A fresh systematic study by a professor of systematic theology and the director of the Center for Hispanic Studies at Concordia Seminary, St. Louis, Missouri. The author examines five models for understanding sanctification from the perspective of "Spirit Christology."

Sasse, Hermann. "On the Doctrine of the Holy Spirit." Pages 200–222 in *Letters to Lutheran Pastors*, volume 3: *1957–1960*. Edited by Matthew C. Harrison. St. Louis: Concordia, 2015.

Written in 1960, a leading confessional Lutheran theologian engages the place of the doctrine of the Holy Spirit in Lutheran theology. He notes that contemporary Christians tend to seek the Spirit where He is not to be found. The Spirit has bonded Himself to the external Word and so is not to be found in personal religious subjectivity or in human techniques to manipulate a crowd. There is a need to discern and "test the spirits" by the Scriptures, for not every movement attributed to the Holy Spirit is of Him.

Schaibley, Robert W. "Spiritual Gifts." *Lutheran Quarterly* 3 (1989): 423–41.
Exegetical and theological examination of spiritual gifts with special attention to the use of "spiritual gift inventories."

Silcock, Jeffrey G. "Luther on the Holy Spirit and His Use of God's Word." Pages 294–309 in *The Oxford Handbook of Martin Luther's Theology*. Edited by Robert Kolb et al. Oxford: Oxford University Press, 2004.
The Australian Luther scholar Jeffrey Silcock provides a finely crafted introduction to Luther's understanding of the indissoluble bond between Word and Spirit, demonstrating that God deals with us inwardly (faith and other spiritual gifts) by the outward use of the Means of Grace. The external is the basis for the internal. "The oral Word and the written Word belong together because in and through both the Holy Spirit communicates and mediates Jesus Christ the savior who is the chief content of the Bible" (302). Silcock also reminds us that "strictly speaking, Christians do not 'possess' the Spirit, but the Spirit 'possesses them' " (305).

Tepker, Howard. "The Holy Spirit." Pages 519–622 in volume 1 of *Confessing the Gospel: A Lutheran Approach to Systematic Theology*. Edited by Samuel H. Nafzger et al. St. Louis: Concordia, 2017.
A careful, systematic exposition of the person and work of the Holy Spirit that begins with the Old Testament and moves through the New Testament into church history. A section on "The Extraordinary Gifts of the Spirit Today" treats contemporary questions surrounding Pentecostalism and the Charismatic Movement. "Spiritual gifts shall never—in theory or practice—rival the Gospel and sacraments as the definitive signs of God's mercy to human creatures" (616).

Wrogemann, Henning. *Intercultural Theology*. Volume Two: *Theology of Missions*. Translated by Karl E. Böhmer. Downers Grove, IL: InterVarsity Press, 2018.
Wrogemann is a leading German missiologist. Chapter 15, "Mission Theological Profiles in Pentecostal Churches and Movements" (235–62), provides a concise overview of the rise of Pentecostalism and its missionary impulses. In his "A Critical Appraisal," Wrogemann notes that "demonological and pneumatological interpretations are a point of entry for all kinds of irrationality" (257). Wrogemann's work gives evidence of substantial field research and engagement with the scholarly literature.

INDEX OF SCRIPTURE REFERENCES

Romans